)))

*Imagination and
the Nature of Choice*

(((

G.L.S.SHACKLE

(((

Imagination

)))

and the

(((

Nature of

)))

Choice

(

Edinburgh University Press

© G.L.S.Shackle 1979
Edinburgh University Press
22 George Square, Edinburgh

ISBN 0 85224 357 X

Set in Monotype Bembo
by Speedspools, Edinburgh
and printed in Great Britain by
R.& R.Clark Ltd
Edinburgh

(

Contents

Preface vii

)))
Preface
(((

I SEEK HERE to show the essential nature of choice as discernible in men's most direct, inescapable and imperious intuitions. What a man most directly and immediately knows is his own thought. For Descartes the fact of thought was the proof of his being. A thought (in an encompassing sense: perception, intellection, emotion, imagination, decision) takes place and yields place in an indivisible unity of transience. The transience of thought is our intuition of time. Does not one thought's transience summon another and this other yet another so that transience suggests succession? What formal frame do we conceive for the succession of thoughts and of moments? It is the linear calendar, the calendar axis, the notion of time-to-come. What can fill that frame? Can its content be observed by an eye-witness? If not, can its content be inferred from what is present to us, the content of the present moment of actuality with its traces, records and memories of time past? If it can be so inferred, then the content of time-to-come is merely a part of the same existent which we cognize in the present, it is essentially one with that present and with all the content of time past, it is implied in its antecedents, it is determinate from eternity to eternity. If so, what is choice? Is choice no more than the recognition of necessity? Is the study of choice the study merely of mechanism, of the operation of all-encompassing causation? Is thought itself, including the business of choice, the determinate effect of cause? If we repudiate this view, do we reject cause? Choice itself, unless it is wholly ineffective, unless it makes no difference, unless it is otiose, insignificant and negligible, must be a cause. Choice, if its nature is what our practical instinct suggests, if it is the locus of *ex nihilo* origination, the genesis of a taking-place not wholly implicit in antecedents, must itself be deemed a cause. It must be deemed in some sense and degree an uncaused cause, what I shall call a *beginning*. To elect for choice the meaning of an uncaused cause is to make it unforeknowable. But the sequel of a present choice will itself contain choices, and if these choices to come are to be deemed non-implicit, they and their effect on the sequel of a present choice are also unforeknowable.

If choice is an uncaused cause and the sequel of any choice therefore not foreknowable as something unique, what is the nature of the *effect* of choice? For must not that effect be the incentive for the chooser to engage in the arduous business of deliberative choice? What can choice do for the chooser? It can shift the bounds of the range of rival possible sequels which the chooser can envisage, the skein of imagined sequels which are not blocked by some discernible obstacle. Some such obstacles can be removed only by choice, for they consist in the chooser's not having committed himself to take some steps of action of his own which seem essential to that sequel. In order to imagine and deem possible my winning of a bet, I am obliged to expose myself, by making the bet, to the possibility of losing it. The steps of action to which the chooser must commit himself will be perhaps an exceedingly complex form of bet, a course of action describable only symbolically and in summary form. The sequels to which such commitment gives him imaginative access, the sequels which compose for that choosable course the *imagined*, *deemed possible*, will be a skein of sequels not limited in number by any essential or inherent principle. The only stop to the business of imagining further variants is the deadline for decision. The arrival at that deadline, therefore, will leave him with an incomplete and essentially uncompletable list of possible sequels, a skein ever-extensible though bounded. If, when we pursue such a line of thought, we see choice as the genesis of non-implicit history, as the origin *ne plus ultra* of history created from moment to moment rather than suffered or enacted in passive obedience to circumstance and reason, we are saying that choice is not in the first place mere calculation but work of imagination, the poet's essential deed. Choice, if so, is made amongst products of the chooser's thought. Then the central enigma for the analyst of choice is the chooser's mode of comparison of rival skeins of rival possibilities of which he is himself the author.

My theme thus avers that choice, if its nature is that of a *beginning*, is necessarily made amongst skeins of rival conceptions of the sequel of action. This rivalry implies unknowledge. How does the chooser replace, for each rival, the claim to be adjudged certain truth, which its circumstance of rivalry denies it? In what form does he accord it epistemic standing, a claim to practical consideration? Choice is an exploitation of unknowledge. It allows the chooser to ask himself: What can be the sequel of such-and-such a course? What concerns him in assessing that course is the best and the worst amongst the answers he can conceive and deem possible. Epistemic standing, for the chooser's purpose of gaining access for practical imagination, is *possibility*, freedom from discernible obstruction. Such is my theme.

It may be asked what relation these heresies bear to the received constructions of economic theory. That question has been answered by a critical intellect of the utmost incisive brilliance. Professor S. C. Littlechild, in commenting on my lecture 'Imagination, Formalism and Choice', has epitomized my conception of things and related it both to to-day's 'mainstream' of neo-classical theory and to the subjectivism stemming from the work of Ludwig von Mises and F. A. von Hayek, the modern exponents and creators of the 'Austrian' school. Professor Littlechild's paper 'From radical subjectivism to radical subversion' seems to me definitive in regard to my work.

In the difficult task of expressing such a theme I have returned to the practice of earlier generations in using capital letters and italic to signal special meanings and linkages of words. Both were used with a lively and efficient freedom in this century by one who had at command every resource of English prose, J. M. Keynes.

I wish to record a profound gratitude to Mark Perlman for his limitless generosity of effort and time in assessing this book when pressed to the utmost by other concerns. He read the manuscript with the closest attention and warned me of the need to make, in this preface, some attempt to signpost my argument in advance. I am deeply grateful to Mrs E. C. Harris for the incomparable help she has given me in proof-reading this book and arranging the material of the index.

G. L. S. Shackle, January 1979.

)))
Thought, transience and time
(((

THE IMMEDIATE KNOWABLE is thought. Descartes' *Cogito* and Russell's *There are thoughts* express this feeling. Thought has an evident definable formal character. A thought is the inseparable unity of an arrival and departure. Its coming and going are one. A thought is a *transient*. The transience of thought is that direct experience which is the prime meaning of time. Thought as transience, transience as time, seems to me the self-establishing basis for an account of the human condition, the Scheme of Things. Transience does not, I think, entail succession, but imperiously suggests it. The abstract notion of a thought which will succeed my present one, and of one which will succeed that successor, and so on endlessly, is the notion of time-to-come. What frame can formal imagination supply to accommodate the notion of an endless succession of transients? We invent an artefact, the calendar-axis. The time-succession is there represented as a line, an axis in a Cartesian reference-frame. Time past is evidenced by memory but such memory is a thought and a thought if it takes place is *present*. Time as succession, past and to come, is an artefact, something inferred, invented to supply a need of present thought. The time-succession, the infinite supposed extension, eternity itself, exists in present thought, is contained in the fleeting passage of the moment, so far as that passage compels the direct intuition of a thinking being.

Thought as the immediate knowable, time as transient thought, are what we name by *the present*. So far as ever its unseizable nature can be suggested in words, it has been held in the flash of genius by

Guillaume de Lorris in the following lines from *Le Roman de la Rose*, so subtly translated by Chaucer:

> The time that passes night and day
> and restlessly travaileth aye
> and steals from us so privily
> that to us seems so certainly
> that in one point it dwelleth ever;
> and certainly it resteth never
> but goes so fast, and passeth aye
> that there's no man that thinken may
> what time is that now present is.
> (*after* Chaucer)

What we know is thought and thought is the present. What *is*, is what present, transient thought tells us of. In this sense, all that *is*, is in the present. We speak of *the present moment*, making particulate something whose essence is its transient passage into a new present. Yet presence (presentness) cuts off and isolates the moment, it is *solitary*.

Our enquiry is into choice. Choice can be only choice of *thoughts of deeds*. We cannot choose what already *is*, that is beyond the reach of choice, it has already chosen itself. Yet the present can embrace thoughts other than, besides, those which seem to report *what is*. Three themes seem to embrace those contents of present thought, those contents of the present, which concern the enquirer into conduct. I shall call them the *News*, the *Scheme*, the *Imagined deemed Possible*:

The News: impressions interpreted as reports from a field.

The Scheme: an account of the geometry (formal coherence) of the field, in terms of the arrangement-possibilities of abstract, typical, constant *elements*. An element here means any building-block which can serve for the delineation of history recorded or imagined.

The Imagined deemed Possible: element-arrangements not presented to thought by the field, but *originated in a strict extreme sense*, that is, created partly *ex nihilo*, by the thinking being.

These terms need elaboration.

The thinking being is the natural hypothesis concerning thought. Such a being appeared to Descartes an entailment of thought. It was conceived by him in distinction from the field. I assume it permissible to understand *res cogitans* and *res extensa* as what I am calling the thinking being and the field.

The supposition of a field distinct from the thinking being, a field conceived as the source of impressions received by him and interpreted by him as reports of takings-place in this field, and thus as capable of tracing parts of the lineaments of this field, has long seemed natural and convenient. It is the nature of the thinking being to exploit the field. Besides the registering of impressions and besides the business of interpreting them in terms of some scheme of understanding of the field, the individual has thoughts concerned with exploiting it. To suppose that he can exploit it is to suppose that he can make a difference to the course of the evolution of its posture, the momentary state of its affairs through the moments of time-to-come. 'Make a difference': this expression implies that the course of affairs in time-to-come can be one thing or another. It suggests that 'of his own motion' he can elect one or other of such courses; that he can in some sense choose. The question, what must here be meant, along many lines, by 'choose' is the subject of my enquiry.

My foregoing passages take one of the two extreme opposing views of the nature of time and its content of history. The question answered in total mutual contradiction by these views concerns the place of the thoughts of men in the history which they cognize. In that history, are these thoughts passive, inert details of a picture which is entire and complete from eternity to eternity, where there are no takings-place because all is already in place from some once-for-all creation, a history where 'time' names only relative location in a co-valid whole? Or by contrast, do thoughts *originate in the extremest sense* a history which has no form or existence until thought summons it, in a character not until then determined, from the void of time-to-come, the void which thus

3

yields a paradoxical all-embracing fertility? The former of these views is the rigorous import of determinism. The second we may call decisionism. Of this I have sought above to give an elemental statement. Do men's thoughts, their work of imagination, bring history out of nothing? If so, the expression 'out of nothing' must be taken seriously and its sense defined.

Determinism deems time an illusion of human thought, and must deem that thought itself in some sense an illusion. Can there then be thoughts which do not *take place*? If they take place, do they not *displace* our consciousness into a new present? The ostensible simplicity which determinism seems to offer appears on examination to be false. For it does not account for consciousness. Consciousness must be separately assumed. The world thus takes on a dual aspect, the aspect of history existing independently of thought, and the aspect of human discovery of this picture bit-by-bit. The determinist view makes time the passive and infertile canvas on which history down to its last detail is painted once for all from beginning to end or from infinity to infinity as a still picture entirely co-existent in all its parts and locations. In such a picture, what is *choice*?

My enterprise here is to draw consequences concerning the nature of choice from some expression of the human entity and predicament, the Scheme of Things. In what terms and by what means can such expression be conceived? Description is comparison and classification. The human entity, the thing whose existence seems testified to by the having thoughts (or at an even more austere spareness and *ne plus ultra*, the having thoughts itself) is unique, incomparable. If it is deemed to belong to a class, it is itself the sole member of that class, and the system contains no other class. Descriptive assignment of the human entity can be only to aspects or elements of the thing itself which we would describe and classify. In this situation there are two modes to which we can resort. There is formalism, and there is poetry. We can allow imagination to construct a frame, essentially like a mathematical system, a set of relations amongst elements which

4

are themselves undefined, or only defined by a circular, mutual self-reference. Then we can declare this formal system to represent for us the thing which is to be described. The association will be in some sense an arbitrary one, but it can claim to rest on some intuitions which themselves lie at the extreme limit of the reach of thought. Alternatively, there is the means of the poet. His intuitions take form in the language of feeling, such feeling as the sense of beauty, or of transcendence. The two modes converge and fuse with one another. We resort to the formal imagination to express the ultimate intuitions. The lines I have quoted from *Le Roman de la Rose* exemplify this act of thought with an unsurpassable perfection. Time itself, unique, incomparable, is delineated by its effect and impression on the thinking being. Time is thought. The formal aspect of thought, surely inescapable, is transience, a term primitive and unanalysable yet immediate as consciousness itself, elementally essential to the very conception of the human entity.

How, save by expressions which draw upon imagination, which hope for a response related in some humble degree to that evoked by poetry, can a writer attain a basis for reasoning about that act which, if any, is the origination of history-to-come by human beings, the act of choice in its elusive complexity? The conception which I have tried to epitomize depends upon a few ideas entirely in discord with much habitual assumption. The language we use from hour to hour presents time as a landscape in which we can move at will, to whose locations we can return, whose features we can *inspect*, not merely reconstruct, repeatedly and at will. In our accustomed speech there is recurrence. The days of the week are places in our round of living, so are the yearly seasons and the times of day. Yet all that *is*, of directly knowable instance, consists in thought, the stuff and content of the unseizable transience of the momentary present. The present is all we know in its being. The present is unique and solitary, cut off from any other thing resembling itself. No 'present' co-exists with any other present. The present in its nature excludes all but itself and contains all in itself, time past and time-to-come. The past is what, by present thought, we recall, or what we reconstruct from appearances, 'traces', which lie before our eyes in the present. The past is the *content* of time past, remembered or inferred. What, then, is time-to-come?

At the outset, in contemplating 'choice', we have to make an election of policy. We can suppose men to be uninvolved in the architecture of their own history, save as enforced dwellers in it. If history was determined in every particular in its whole stretch of finite or infinite extent, at some source outside of that history, at some once-for-all creation, men's thoughts and acts are merely items amongst those particulars. If we name as 'choices' some of those thoughts and acts, we do not, in this determinist view, mean that any such 'choice' or 'chosen' act *makes a difference*. In the determinist elected view, 'choices' are not made, they are mere details of an eternally complete picture. If choices are not made, no circumstances, no data, no values numerical or moral, no causes, can be held responsible for their making. If choices are not made, nothing can influence their making, their making can influence nothing. Choice in the determinist view can be nothing but the name of an illusion. In absolute contrast with a determinism where time is the mere extension accommodating the fixed complete-ness of a narrative, we can elect time as the sole fertility, encom-passing the continuous original creation of the transient present in men's imagination and its taking place in reports from the field in a succeeding present. Such a conception gives to the word choice an import wholly at odds in essential respects with the meaning assigned to it in, for example, the theory of value set out in treatises on economics.

The conception proposed here of thought, transience and time, fused in meaning to describe, by appeal to intuitions, the pre-dicament of human beings, directly confronts us with basic questions concerning what we had best still refer to as choice.

)))
Time as the business of imagination
(((

IMAGINATION, THE SOURCE and business of original thought, is the indispensable resource of non-determinism. The view which supposes history to be uncreated until the present, to be the thing whose creation is the endless and continuous practical business of the present, can make this view the liberator of men only by imposing on them the task of the origination of history. If men are essentially free, they are essentially creative in a fundamental sense. That sense confronts thought with a *ne plus ultra*. *Original*, *origin* and *source*, if their meaning is carried to the extreme, imply a taking-place which, in some respect, has no essential, indispensable, irrepudiable antecedents. Beyond *origin*, in its ultimate reach of meaning, we discern nothing. We are denied, by this meaning, the right to ask what antecedents had this taking-place as a necessary part of their sequel. We are required, by this meaning, to acknowledge takings-place in the present as not mere aspects, only now revealed but eternally existent, of an unchanging unity for which the transient present is an illusion. Takings-place may, in this view, be the expression of thoughts which did not owe their whole form and import to what went before. Such takings-place can *make a difference* to the history which follows them. They can be such as to impose, or to remove, fatal obstacles to some imaginable sequels. Thus such a taking-place, expressing a thought not itself determined by antecedents, can be the beginning of an evolution of affairs made possible by this original, that is, not wholly determined thought. Such a thought and deed is an origin and source of history in our usage of these words, but not in the sense of

7

a once-for-all determining creation. I shall name these originating thoughts, able to occur unheralded in any present, *beginnings*:

> *beginning:* a taking-place not wholly knowable from antecedents no matter how completely themselves known, a taking-place not implicit in antecedents, a taking-place such that the sequel would be different if this taking-place were different, a taking-place thus originating *ex nihilo* some characters of a train of events in history, an *uncaused cause*.

> *beginning* thus defined is a formal abstraction. If we suppose it to be a character of thought, the thinking being becomes the continuous originator of history. Imagination is what we call the source and business of such thought.

There is a condition *sine qua non* for the origination of history in this sense, a condition for the taking-place of *beginnings*. Evidently the time-to-come in which the originated history will take form must be the void. The void of time-to-come is a necessity of my theme. Time which is still to come cannot be filled by reports from the field. In any present it can be filled by each man only by work of imagination. Imagined history-to-come is a means of life, an indispensable tool or ingredient of action to elicit desired reports from the field. It will not serve such a purpose unless it seems, to the chooser of action in pursuit of desired reports, to be exempt from discernible fatal obstacles. If an imagined evolution of his affairs seems to the chooser to be fatally obstructed, effort will be wasted, in his judgement, which seeks to bring it about. Desired reports from the field cannot be looked for along paths which are blocked. Imagined filling of time-to-come must, in order to serve its purpose, be deemed possible. This was our name for the third of the three themes of the present. As a tool of the inescapable task of choosing action, imagination must observe constraints. But imagination is the indispensable and only means. Time-to-come imperiously demands to be filled, it provides the practical business of imagination.

If choice is a beginning in our sense, a taking-place which is in some respects uncaused, and which yet makes a difference to its

8

sequel, the chooser of action who thus views the nature of choice is bound to suppose that the sequel of any present choice of action which he makes will be partly shaped by choices made, by others or himself, in time-to-come, and thus he is bound to acknowledge that such a sequel cannot be seen as a unique path of events. To be interesting, any imagined history-to-come must seem possible, but in the nature of choice it cannot be the sole and unique possible. There must, in principle, be recognition of a skein of plural, rival, possible sequels of any present choice of action. That skein of sequels, its members mutually exclusive rivals, is not given by the field. The view of the nature of choice that we have elected as a means of adopting non-determinism, is wholly at odds with the notion of a set of choosables given ready-made to the chooser by some agency outside his own thought. What I shall call the rival choosables, namely, the courses of action and the sequels associated with them, must in my theme be deemed to be originated by the chooser's self.

In this view, time as the present is concerned with originating possible contents for time-to-come. This is a business of imagination. Why must we say '*possible* contents of time to come' rather than '*the* contents . . .'? If choice is a beginning in our sense, and thus gives to the course of things an impulse divorced in some respects from antecedents and not foreknowable from any knowledge of antecedents no matter how complete, then a recognition by any chooser that there will be making of choices, by others and by himself, in time-to-come entails that his present choice (that is to say *any* actual choice) will have its sequel shaped in part by circumstances which he cannot foreknow. It follows that he *cannot exclude as impossible* all except one such sequel. Many, and we may say infinitely many, distinct and rival sequels which he might imagine would have to be acknowledged by him as *possible*. The content of time-to-come envisaged by the chooser must be a skein of rival possibilities, of rival possible sequels of some course of immediate action on which he might resolve. Such skeins will themselves be rivals of each other, each being made accessible to imaginative experience (to anticipation, a taking-beforehand) by an appropriate course of action resolved upon. Choice is made amongst such courses, each with its skein of indefinitely numerous sequels, each originated by the chooser and not found by him to be fatally epistemically obstructed.

My theme subverts the view of choice as a passive response of the chooser to a set of choosables each fully relevantly specified, finitely numerous and thrust upon him without his participation. Earlier choices of his will have played a part in determining where the edges of the possible are for him now located. But within these epistemic bounds ('possible' is a judgement made by himself in the light of his knowledge of the field and of himself) he is free to originate the choosable entities, the mutually rival acts within reach and their respective skeins of envisageable (practically supposable, not-impossible) sequels. Choices in this view are, in their full burden and complexity of meaning, the genesis of history from moment to moment, a *ne plus ultra* of explanatory thought.

)))
The source and nature of the
rival choosables
(((

CHOICE, AS THE name of a business of thought, seems to have three formal essentials:

A set of entities distinct from each other.

A specialty which can be conferred on any one but only one of these entities.

A source and mode of this conferment.

I mean by specialty a distinguishing mark or standing. In stating the formal essentials we need say nothing except that this mark must be exclusively conferred on only one of the set of entities, which in respect of it are thus rivals. I shall call them *rival choosables*. The statement of the formal frame leaves entirely open a number of questions whose answers are part of the description of the human predicament, part of the view we take of the Scheme of Things decreed for us. These questions converge upon one question, the essential nature of the rival choosables. I shall suggest that choice is necessarily amongst thoughts, that these are thoughts concerning deeds to be done, moves to be made, by the chooser in time-to-come however immediate, and that these thoughts are such that when the problem of choice has been resolved, the result is a *beginning* in my sense.

It seems evident that choice cannot be made amongst reports from the field. The chooser has a salutary *practical conscience*, which broadly forbids self-deception. It does so in the interest of the survival of the chooser. Reports from the field, composing from moment to moment the scene offered to his senses, are by assumption not of his making. In expressing the chooser's experience of the present as consisting of three themes, we supposed that he takes sense-impressions as evidence of a field, *res extensa*, and that these impressions report what *already is*. Choice cannot be made amongst facts, they have already been chosen, or have chosen themselves. Choice requires *rivals*. Choice is choice of a course of action able to be followed by a desired sequel in the evolution of history-to-come. The rivalry of the choosables must thus consist in a claim of each to be able to lead to reports from the field, in times-to-come, which will record the desired history as actual, as an account, at those times, of what then is. The choosables are thus required to have double nature. Each must aspire to the occupancy of one and the same stretch of time-to-come, yet all must co-exist in the chooser's choosing thoughts, his *present* thoughts. Only thoughts, not facts, can possess this double essential capacity. Choice is necessarily made amongst works of thought, of imagination. Choice is made amongst thoughts originated by the chooser.

In our daily discourse, in unconsidered language, we speak of choosing amongst things, physical objects which exist or are conceived to be going to exist. We choose this house rather than that. But plainly what we choose is the intention to buy, or to live in, this house rather than that. The field does not, cannot, offer *existent rivals*. It can only suggest rival evolutions of affairs. What is *suggestion*? It is the touching of the keys of an instrument, not an instrument of unchanging conformation and design, but one continually developed and modified by the incoming reports and by the endeavour to interpret to-day's, this moment's, report in the light of the Scheme which has grown from all earlier reports. Suggestion is the play of the new on the accepted. Is it not here, in the response which the thinking being makes, out of his intellectual and emotional resources, by a flash of sometimes inspired origination, of truly *ex nihilo* re-forming of ideas, that we can see the cutting of the determinist thread, the entry into history, at any present moment, of thoughts and takings-place not implied in their antecedents, the entry of undetermined arrangements of the abstract elements in which the chooser sees the basis of all his experience?

The field is taken to be a self-consistent whole, the reports which the chooser receives in any present are compatible co-existents, the Scheme by which they are interpreted is a coherent unity, or at least aspires to be such, there is in all this content of thought no rivalry at the heart of things. Rivalry can find a place only in the contemplation of the void of time-to-come, which will necessarily be filled by men's choices and their inter-actions, but whose content does not in any present exist until men's choices have begun it.

In these paragraphs above, we have sought to answer a first question about the rival choosables: Whence are they presented to the chooser? They are the products of his *original* thought, his re-assembly, in configurations never realized in the field in its past, of the elements into which he resolves his basic scheme of that field. These re-assemblies can be rivals for the same stretch of time-to-come, but they must conform to the scheme of Nature and of human nature which he has evolved, they must be exempt from discerned fatal obstacles, they must be *possible* in his judgement.

To propose an answer to one question necessarily raises others and still others. I have been suggesting that origination of histories-to-come takes the form of compositions of elements, building-blocks of a scheme of the field and of its *potentiae*. What characters and classifications we can assign to the elements is an inescapable question, but it must wait. We have been proceeding from the broadest aspects of the 'receptacle', the setting of the business of choice, towards the fibre of the business itself. How do the rival imagined histories-to-come allow and call for an act of choice?

The imagined histories designed for filling time-to-come must seem to the chooser not impossible. But this adjudged capacity-to-be-realized has three separately indispensable bases. Any such history claiming a part in the business of choice is required to conform to Nature and human nature, it must respect the principles of the architecture of the field. Besides this, since 'time-to-come' takes its start from the chooser's present, a history for that time must be an evolution starting from the situation at that present, as the chooser sees it. We may epitomize these first two bases as conformity to the nature and the posture of things. But if any imagined history is to bear upon choice, choice also must bear upon it. The possibility of each such history must depend upon the chooser's making an appropriate choice of action. The histories must be looked on as *sequels* of action. There thus presents itself an inter-lacing of questions of the utmost subtlety and complexity. We wish to consider how an action can be said to have imagined sequels when those sequels are plural rivals excluding each other. But before this we must ask: Since 'action' and 'sequel' both stand for contents of time-to-come, what divides and distinguishes action from sequel? What is the operation and effect of the act of choice, within the chooser's thought? In what exact manner does his choice affect the possibility he adjudges to an imagined history? These questions concern the organization of the chooser's expectational thought. But their answers rest perhaps upon the answers we give to prior questions. We have not yet asked what is the chooser's incentive for assuming the burden of making a choice? What does the making of a choice do for the chooser? What *difference* does the making of a choice make to the chooser?

What difference can the choosing of one course of action rather than another make, immediately and directly, to the chooser? It cannot instantly bring reports from the field different in the case of one chosen course from those of another. What is immediately (in the strict sense) and necessarily affected by the act of choice is the chooser's state of mind, let us say his state of thought; in especial his state of imagination. For choice is a poising of thought. The chooser's act of choice modifies, gives a particular character to the posture of things in his present. It gives to the material things within his disposal an *orientation*, an envisaged purpose, a coherent function and intended use. It has this effect also on the suggestions for action that he will make to other individuals whom he can direct or influence. In these ways his choice will remove what would have been discernible obstacles from some evolutions of

14

affairs, some paths of history relevant to his interest, for example by allocating means and operations essential to those courses of events, the absence of which would have blocked them. Choice *makes seemingly possible* some imagined histories-to-come. In doing so it denies possibility to imagined histories conflicting with the one in question. All this it does *in the chooser's thought*. Choice allows the chooser to anticipate ('take beforehand') some unfoldings of affairs and precludes his supposition of others. If the effect of choice is to allow the chooser to envisage as possible some desired variants of history-to-come, what is the essence of the act of choice which gives it such a power? Its vital nature is commitment. Choice is a resolve, a moral and not merely an intellectual act. Choice erects a structure of intentions, any abandonment of which will be hurtful to the chooser in some degree. In the act of choice, the chooser in some degree stakes his own self-esteem.

In the conception of the nature of choice, which I have been here proposing, the central notions are those of the origination of the rival choosables by the chooser, in the strict sense of the forming of ideas not wholly implicit in antecedents; the constitution of each such rival by a skein of histories-to-come imagined and deemed possible, but themselves mutually rival; of the constraint of the work of imagination, in the business of composing histories-to-come, by the test of epistemic possibility imposed by the chooser's salutary practical conscience; of the character of this test, requiring the conformity of imagined histories to the nature and the 'present' posture of things; and of the essential involvement, in that posture of things, of the chooser's chosen intended moves or steps of action; and finally, of the nature of choice as private moral commitment, the staking of moral coherence and self esteem, in some degree, on the actual taking of a series of steps in immediate or near time-to-come. This conception of the nature of choice raises questions which we may tentatively list below.

Origination of histories-to-come, conceived as the non-implicit arrangement of elements whose individual nature reflects a scheme of geometry of the field and is suggested by reports from the field is a notion impelling us to consider what characters in common such building-blocks may be supposed to have such as would entitle us to name them together as *elements*. What kinds of thing (what kinds of thought) are the elements, how suggested, how evolving under the influence of reports from the field? What governs the fitting-together of the elements, what sequences or associations do we suppose to be epistemically possible? What constraints on the architecture of imagined histories are inherent in the nature we assign to the elements?

Epistemic possibility, the absence, from the chooser's thought and knowledge, of fatal obstacles to any imagined course of affairs, is the necessary condition for that imagined course to be able to affect his choice. What form can such obstacles take? Can they be illuminatingly classified so that the connection between steps of action open to the chooser, and the removal of some such obstacles in the particular cases of some desired histories-to-come can be subjected to general principles? In what detailed manner does epistemic possibility gather variant and rival histories-to-come into skeins which can be envisaged as the *sequel* of particular courses of action open to the chooser?

Are there non-fatal envisageable obstacles, difficulties of conceiving a particular course of affairs as realizable? Can the degree of any such difficulty be given meaning? Can the degrees of this difficulty and that, affecting different sequels, be compared, ordered or measured on some scale?

On what principle, by what test, can *course of action* be divided and distinguished from *imagined sequel of action*? Are not both of them work of imagination? Do we find this test in the chooser's meaning for *commitment*, limiting it to steps of action which seem unquestionably within his reach?

But what is a *step of action*, or a *course of action* composed of a sequence or configuration of such steps? How closely must a step be defined? Is not any envisageable step a *class* of (precise) actions? Must not step of action, course of action, move, be conceived as symbols each reified and having only simplified and imprecise content?

If the sequel ascribed to each available course of action is a skein of mutually exclusive variants, what influences or constrains the number of such variants? How many distinct sequels do we suppose the chooser to envisage? Is the number of sequels, for any one course of action, in any way essentially limited in principle? If not, what is the bearing of the *uncompletable* nature of such a skein or list of sequels, on the chooser's mode of assigning and expressing the epistemic standing of any such sequel?

By *epistemic standing* I mean the claim, accorded by the chooser to any hypothesis, to be taken seriously, given *audience* in his business of choice. What can be the nature of judgements of epistemic standing? My proposal is that such judgements or assessments concern possibility, absence of discernible obstacles. What question does a judgement of epistemic standing answer, and what disabilities are imposed on some formal modes of answering it? These questions are the intended themes of following chapters.

)))
The Scheme
(((

THE NOTIONS OF *choice* and *cause* seem essential to each other. If choice is what I have called a *beginning*, a taking-place in an individual's thought which *makes a difference*, so that the subsequent course of affairs is not quite what it would have been, or perhaps is momentously not what it would have been, without that thought, then we are supposing choice to inform in some degree and manner the course of things, to have an effect on the form which history takes. Choice, if so, is a cause, in more than one of the meanings which have been assigned to that word. For it is in that case both a proximate cause, the immediately antecedent and conjoined circumstance, and also an ultimate cause, a cause itself uncaused, an *ex nihilo* origination; if we like, the flash of inspiration. If these foregoing suppositions are elected, the notion of cause is part of the notion of effective, inceptive, originative choice, powerful choice in contrast to sterile and passive response to circumstance and tastes. How can choice be powerful unless it is a cause with effects? But equally, choice is indispensable to cause, except in so far as there are 'random' events in Nature. Random events, like inspired thoughts, can be beginnings in our technical sense. In so far as Nature is informed by constant principles, Nature is determinate. If there were no beginnings; if there were, for example, no heritable mutations occurring, as seems to be supposed, unforeknowably; then Nature would constitute a determinate world. What of the human world, that, perhaps, extreme outlier of terrestrial Nature? If all thoughts were the calculable upshot of antecedents (calculable, could those antecedents be known) then the human world, being a part of the determinate natural world, would also be in every way determinate. Where then would be the need for a notion of cause? In one sense, no doubt, we can say that a window of a house is caused by the house. If there were no house, there would be no window. But equally, we can discern circumstances in whose absence there would be no house; and so on, indefinitely. Perhaps we could say that in a wholly determinate world, *cause* would be circular, like the definitions given in the dictionary. Cause must have a beginning. Cause must not involve an infinite regress of causes or it will find itself claiming to be its own cause. It must arrive ultimately, if it is to be meaningful, at *uncause*. In so far as uncause finds its embodiment only in choice, choice is essential to cause.

My theme maintains that if choices are beginnings, if they are in some sense *ex nihilo* originations, and if the chooser can, by his bodily actions and above all by his suggestions made to others, give effect in the field to these original thoughts; if the field is so constituted that it can give audience to the chooser's initiatives so that they can make a difference, so that what takes place in the field will be this, or this – according to the chooser's chosen course of action; then, by a strange paradox, choice will be able only to start ripples whose effect can be seen as confined in some degree but not determined. If choice is effective, its effects can be only most uncertainly, vaguely and elusively foreknown, and beyond some near horizon (near in terms of the human life-span or concern with affairs) cannot be foreknown at all. This is the paradox of choice: if effective, we cannot know what it will effect. If we can in principle know the content of time-to-come then that content is beyond our reach to influence or inform in any way. If such determinism is the truth, we are the deluded slaves of necessity, able perhaps to foreknow what we are obliged to do and what pattern of history those doings will contribute to, but having no claim to call those deeds our own. Men, in that case, are mere tools of fate. My theme is a search for some of the consequences of rejecting such determinism. It does not thereby elect anarchy or total disintegration of history and affairs. If choice is effective, it must work in a textured world, a world where takings-place are as it were consanguineous and not wholly alien to each other, are held together in threads and skeins. If choice is to be the pursuit of desires and ambitions, the chooser must have in mind some notions of *what can follow what*. He must view the world as a pattern of natural barriers rather than of narrow and prescribed tracks. What *can* take place, he must suppose, is bounded but not prescribed.

What *can* follow what is the subject-matter and content of the principles of Nature which men distil from their impressions from the field. So long as they are seen chiefly as providing technologies, the principles may impinge little on each other in men's thoughts. But conflicts between them will even then be puzzling and confusing. When there is time for thought to be free from the needs of survival, when the search for pure insight is illumined and inspired by a search for formal conceptual beauty, the principles must be brought together by a system, an embracing theory where many principles formerly thought of as independent are seen as illustrations of a more powerful and far-reaching principle. It is not only non-human Nature that must be embraced by the Scheme which is to interpret the impressions into News and be resolved into elements as building-blocks for the Imagined, deemed Possible, the originated possible sequels of available choices of action. For what can follow what, in a narrower sense than that of general physical principle, will depend also on the orientations, the supposed intentions, which the chooser adjudges to other people. These also may seem to him to be subject to some principles, so that 'What can follow what' will need for its practical and applicable discernment a Scheme embracing human as well as non-human Nature. The Scheme, the general interpretive and originative tool or reference-book, must surely in some form be constructed and used by every individual, each designing his own according to his own experience and education.

)))
Elements
(((

I HAVE SOUGHT to show that *choice as origination* involves the notion of *cause uncaused*, of a cut in the fabric of governance of the present, and of the history-to-come, by the past. Yet choice concerns itself with *res extensa*, with a field supposed by the thinking being to exist outside his thought. It is takings-place in this field, or the receiving of reports of such takings-place, that are the matter and receptacle of his ambitions, his ends. Is it not then a fundamental problem for us, enquirers into choice, to explain how history-to-come can be imagined by the chooser, *originated* in diverse mutually rival forms, yet be concerned with, and therefore composed of, entities in some sense given, the things which the chooser, interpreting in some fashion his received impressions, judges to exist or to take place in the field? How can there be untramelled imagination, free to bring out of nothing, in some sense, the course of affairs in time-to-come, yet also a field with a stable constitution and principles of Nature, working in settled ways of its own? What will reconcile these two ostensible incompatibles? The answer to this question seems to me to be *alphabetic*. The letters of an alphabet are constant, essentially invariant against changes of context and circumstance, yet they are capable of embodiment in language-constructs of strictly *endless* variety and novelty. The alphabetic particles of imagined history-to-come, which in my theme is the stuff of the rival choosables, need a name and I propose to call them *elements*. Some notion, then, must be proposed of the nature and essential formal character of *elements* in this sense.

What have elements to *do*? What is their function or duty in the business of choice? They are required as the means of description of the attractive or repellent in the content of the Imagined, deemed Possible. What is the chooser's concern with history-to-come? For the detached observer, this concern is the survival and the publicly visible prosperity of the chooser. For the detached observer, all the points of the calendar-axis are equally valid and their content equally 'objective'. But the chooser cannot experience takings-place, or attained situations, whose *entelechy* or actual existence is located in time-to-come. For the chooser, those takings-place cannot in his present be actual. What can be present to him is his imagination of those takings-place. It is the anticipation of these takings-place, their existence by *dunamis*, by *potentia*, in his present thought, that is the incentive for his making the originative efforts and the moral resolutive effort involved in choice. In order to imagine sequels to an available present choice, in order thus to experience an anticipative enjoyment (salutary through its possible inducement of action), or an anticipative apprehension (salutary through its warning against exposure to disaster) the chooser needs an alphabet and a language with which to give form to the possible sequels of a choice. The elements must, then, have in some sense an emotive content or at least an emotive capacity or potential. They must be ideas attractive in themselves individually or when they are suitably combined. Or they must be alarming in themselves or in arrangements which the chooser cannot exclude. If this power of inducing feelings is to reside in symbols which describe regions or features of the field, the *res extensa*, they must include in such description a statement of the significance with which these features are endowed by the chooser, a statement of how he imagines these features as serving or disserving his purposes. The description built up with these symbols, with these elements, must be informed with a teleology, what we are calling an orientation. The description must consist of intentions concerning the use of material objects or systems or the services of people, or it must state the significance for the chooser

22

of the supposed existence of such systems or the readiness of such people to render services, or it must record a stage attained in the realization of some ambition or the execution of some enterprise. If the elements are to fulfil these requirements, they must be, within a wide meaning, documentary. Their imagined visible aspect must be that of such things as financial accounts, written contracts, published criticism (in the real sense), electoral results, experiences describable in terms of places and persons, descriptions of technological constructions. The elements must serve to spell out the chooser's ends and his perceived hazards, in an alphabet of readable items with referends in the field.

The notion of elements in our usage flows from the following formal essentials:

1. They must serve to describe the oriented field.
2. They must be composable in endlessly various arrangements.
3. Their attainable arrangements will be constrained by the chooser's oriented present situation and by time-lapse to come.

These statements need some elaboration:

1. The word 'describe' implies classification. To describe an entity, an idea, is to place it in one box out of a plurality of boxes each of which is an answer (the answers differing from box to box) to some one question, such as 'What colour?', 'How large?' 'Possessing what capabilities'. 'How resolute?' *et cetera*. A description will often require the answering of many such questions. The elements must be *classificatory boxes*. They must be symbols.

The 'field' is, for the thinking being, the supposed source of the impressions which he interprets into the News. It is such reports, *reports-to-come*, which he envisages in the teleological act of choice. The chooser is concerned with the field, he is concerned with its *potentiae*. Thus the content of the elements must refer to the field. The elements, in so far as they include notions of material objects or takings-place, must be deemed subject to natural principles, those which are

C   23

embodied in the chooser's Scheme of the field.

'Oriented': The description of the field is not merely that of the physical and technological characters and spatial arrangement of its material objects and human 'crew', even when this catalogue includes an account of the skills and propensities of those people so far as the chooser knows them. The field must be described in its capacity as the tool or the 'receptacle' of his ambitions. For this, it requires in effect as many descriptions as the chooser has distinct available courses of action in mind. Each such course implies and constitutes an orientation of the field, a view of it, an insight into its *potentiae*, as a means to desired sequels and as the source of the threat of counter-desired sequels. Accordingly the elements must be capable of describing the field as a *means to the chooser's ends*.

2. 'composable': The elements must be capable of being assembled freely, like the *tesserae* of a mosaic, not under rigid dictation by their form like the pieces of a jigsaw. This freedom of composition, however, follows necessarily from the nature of choice as we are supposing it. Material things will interact according to natural principles when brought together, as tools act on the substance which is being fabricated, or as seeds germinate in damp soil. But the applying of one thing to another is a decision of the individual, an act of origination of history. Natural principles are brought into action by choices whose nature we are supposing to be that of *beginnings*. Again, the interactions of individuals can be ripples started by the chooser. Natural processes and the acts of individuals, seen from the standpoint of our chooser, are symbolic or typical entities set in a matrix of his own and others' choices, set in the mortar of these choices and as capable of being assembled into endlessly various forms as bricks are capable of being assembled into endlessly various buildings.

3. 'constrained by the chooser's present situation and by time-

lapse to come': At any present, the material means of action are arranged in some pattern as the upshot of past history up to that present. The acts open to the chooser in bringing these means to act on each other are infinitely various, but various only within bounds set by the present physical configuration of these means and by the natural physical principles which govern speeds of movement and re-action. Diffusion of ideas, transmission of suggestions (including 'commands') of action to others, are constrained (variously in mode and degree at various historical epochs) by technology and the state of education and opinion. The situations, states of affairs, which can be deemed attainable from a given oriented 'present' situation, within a specified time-lapse, will depend on the character of the present situation and the speeds of transformation deemed possible.

What, then, are *elements*? They are symbolic types of configurations of means both material and human, each element being able to engender any one of a great diversity of other such elements as a further step on a desired or counter-desired path of affairs. An element is a seed capable of germination and of thus bearing an unlike seed, and so of forming a link in a chain of evolution of affairs, one chain out of an infinity in which the original element is capable of being a link. Such elements themselves are products of the chooser's imagination at work on the cumulative suggestions offered by the News from the field.

)))
The Imagined, deemed Possible
(((

W E H A V E S U P P O S E D the thinking being to have thoughts of three distinguishable kinds concerned with choice of action. His end in all thinking concerned with choice is to exploit the circumstances presented by the field. If circumstances are to be exploited they must be potentially known to the chooser. They must have been reported and interpreted. What he can hope to exploit, to use to his advantage, the thing to which he can hope to *make a difference* in his own interest, is what is described by the *scheme* by which the field has come to be represented in his thoughts. The Scheme describes the nature and the posture of the field, it describes what the field is capable of in general and how its components are disposed in his present. Choice is the act of completing the Scheme as a description of the present by orienting it by means of the chooser's own intended steps of action. The three themes of the chooser's thought, in this conception, are the reports from the field, which I have been calling the News; the gradually integrated Scheme, which describes what the field is like in its principles, its fibre; and the Imagined, deemed Possible, the evolution which, within the principles of nature, of the field, can take this form or that according to the choice of action now to be made by the chooser. That evolution, even for any one choice of action, cannot be envisaged as unique, for the chooser cannot discern some fatal obstacle to all but one of the histories-to-come which he can imagine as sequels to that choice. What choice can do is to set in one place or another the bounds of the possible, within which imagined sequels are required to lie, if they are to bear, even potentially, upon choice. What then do we mean by *possible*?

Possibility is a significance of knowledge, a character of the chooser's particular state of knowledge in his present. If his knowledge of the answer to some question were in some way guaranteed to him to be perfect and complete, nothing concerning that answer would be possible, except the answer itself in its uniqueness. Plural possibilities entertained by the chooser imply unknowledge in some degree. However we are ascribing to the chooser a view, tacit or explicit, consciously held or unconsciously acted on, concerning time-to-come and its content, namely that this content is not only unknown to him but unknowable, because its form and character, the history-to-come which can be supposed to fill that time, waits to be created, to be *originated*, by choices to be made, now and in time-to-come, by himself and others. *Plural possibility* thus flows, not from the chooser's mere unknowledge of something knowable, but from the unknowability of the non-existent. The chooser's unknowledge reflects the ultimate nature of time and the field. This is the supposition which seems to be imposed on us by our election of the non-determinist policy of thought, and our location of the source of non-determinism in the nature of choice.

For the chooser, nonetheless, what concerns him is his unknowledge whatever its source. Unknowledge expresses itself as the need to entertain plural rival answers to some question. The need to entertain them is imposed by the chooser's having no epistemic means of excluding all but one of the plural answers. He cannot discern, in each of these answers, some fatal obstacle to its emerging as the truth. Possibility, for the chooser, is the absence of discernible fatal obstacles. 'Possible' would be an empty term if takings-place of some kinds were not judged to be *impossible*. If every history-to-come which the chooser could invent were deemed by him capable of being realized, the word possible, applying then to everything imaginable, would have no bearing on the business of choice, it would have no part to play in the chooser's thought. If *possible* is to be a useful and needed term, some things which thought can conjure must be deemed impossible, there must be bounds to the possible. Yet possibility must be in some manner dependent on choice, choice must be able to make a difference to the bounds of the possible, if choice itself is not to be empty. If the plural rival histories-to-come, which the chooser envisages, to which he accords possibility, are given independently of his choice, that choice is needless, otiose and ineffective. We need to distinguish from each other *general* and *special* possibility. *General possibility* is a category open to receive all histories-to-come which the chooser may imagine and to which he can discern no fatal obstacles except such as would arise from his own choice of action and, for any one such history, could be all removed by a different choice. General possibility is still a category limited by the conditions of the chooser's *present*. General possibility we deem to depend not only on the nature of the field, its inherent and enduring principles as these are perceived by the chooser, but also on the configuration of the field in the chooser's present, the contingent arrangement of its parts, in so far as this does not depend on his own intended action, any action to which his choice could commit him. *Special possibility* is confined to the imagined histories-to-come which the chooser conceives as rival hypothetical sequels of some one course of action of his own, and which are unobstructed by any discerned obstacles on condition of his taking that course.

General possibility is subject to the essential nature of the field, as the chooser conceives it. General possibility inheres in the chooser's Scheme, subject to the contingent state of the field in his present. The bounds of general possibility are thus set by two sorts of consideration. If we ask whether some specified state of affairs assigned to some named calendar-date in time-to-come, falls within general possibility, the answer will depend on the state of affairs in the chooser's present, from which any process of transformation would have to start, and on the speeds of transformation which the essential nature of things seems to allow. The further question the chooser needs to ask, is what course of action on his own part is pre-supposed when *effective* possibility, special possibility, is assigned to the attainment of the specified state of affairs at the specified date. The matter can be expressed by saying that the *effective* starting point includes amongst its characters the chooser's chosen course of action in his thoughts, his intended course, to which a particular choice commits him. The effective starting-point encompasses, in its sufficient description, not only the publicly visible arrangement of things but also their orientation, their intended use in a coherent policy, in the chooser's thought.

The notion of orientation of the material means and potential human activities which the action-chooser can dispose of is highly useful in our theme. The *potentiae* of an assemblage of things and engageable persons, its claim to be an organization, a system, a *tool* of a complex and powerful kind, depend upon some action-chooser's intention, more or less explicit, more or less exact, detailed and complete, to use this assemblage for purposes which he has formed or adopted. Orientation is essential to the notion of *value* of material things or systems. There is no *intrinsic* value. Value rests ultimately on capability to serve a purpose, and things which are being thought of as serving a purpose are thereby oriented in the particular individual's thought. Evidently an identified thing may have many orientations in the thought of one individual, and these may be rival orientations which exclude each other. The same identified object, or the same class of objects, may have orientations in the thoughts of other individuals. The notion of exchange-value, which has occupied so much of the attention of economists, is an attempt to summarize the effect of the complex inter-action of rival orientations entertained by one or many individuals. A man who values a particular thing more highly, in terms of his own possessions, than any other persons who are aware of this thing can improve his resources by exchange. Thus the notions of exchange, and of exchange-value, are important adjuncts to the theme of choice.

Our account of the concept of the Imagined, deemed Possible, must include one further question of high complexity where our conclusions will have essential bearings on our theme. How far into time-to-come do we suppose the chooser to extend his imagined sequels of present action? That action must be supposed to have a less and less easily discernible effect, to make less and less apparent difference, the more remote the calendar-date considered. But also, the degree of concern or interest which the chooser feels in the situations, or their transformations, at remote epochs will doubtless often diminish with increase of that remoteness, whether or not he supposes that they can be discernibly affected by his present choice of action. Beyond some distance into time-to-come, he may acknowledge a *time-horizon*. In different matters there may be several such horizons. What considerations will bear on the choice of these distances? In what sense or by what means can they be stated, measured or compared? What are the implications of the chooser's acknowledging horizons, for our theme as a whole?

The idea of time-horizon is inseparable from our conception of the nature and source of the chooser's unknowledge of the sequel of his choice. That unknowledge is unknowledge of the non-existent. Time-to-come, in our elected meaning of choice, is the void waiting to be filled by men's constrained imaginations interacting in their committed endeavours to realize their hopes. The sequels of any contemplated course of action, sequels imagined and deemed possible by any chooser, must branch and proliferate as he considers times more and more remote from his present. For the only constraints upon that diverging proliferation are the limitations imposed by the principles of Nature and the nature and capacities of humanity upon the speeds of transformation of one visible situation or one state of men's thoughts into another. Choice, in our theme, is a *beginning*, a taking-place containing an element of the unheralded, the unpresaged, an element exempt from governing antecedents, springing with absolute novelty *ex nihilo*. The number and the timing of such choices is essentially and necessarily unforeknowable. What then is to provide any bounds to the spreading plain of possible courses which affairs might follow from the visible situation of any present moment?

The only limitation is the *texture* of the evolution of history, and the capacities and the resources which the chooser sees in himself and in his reach in the present, and in what may be suggested to him by the past conduct of others concerning their ambitions and desires. By consultation of these seen or hinted circumstances and these received principles, he may be able, for any contemplated course of action of his own, to locate in various dimensions the edges of the possible for the sequels of his own action. But within those edges, the members of the skein of rival imagined sequels will in remoter contemplated times lose their identities and entangle or finally fuse with each other. But more than this. The skeins of sequels ascribed to different present choices will overlap each other, so that the shift of the bounds of the possible, effected by the choice of one course of immediate action rather than another, will lose part of its meaning and distinctness. When the chooser contemplates times remote enough for this, his imaginative power has reached its practical limit. To look beyond is then impossible. This is the time-horizon in its ineluctable form.

This is what, in the ultimate nature of the Scheme of Things, in the logic of that Scheme according to the premises we have elected (the making of some election being inescapable) imposes an horizon on men's expectations, upon the skeins of rival originations of history-to-come which each must compose. But within this logical ultimate the practical limits will surely be much more easily recognized by the chooser himself and by the would-be analyst of his thoughts. The number of rival possible sequels of a somehow-specified course of action may in principle be indefinitely great. We shall ask below what is to confine it or end the potentially infinite process of adding to its number. But the number of rival sequels which can in any sense be held in view and compared, on one hand, and the complexity and time-extension of each such sequel, on the other, must surely be functions of each other. The former will decrease, we may suppose, as the latter become greater. To seek to push out the expectational horizon is to increase both the plurality of the sequels and the elaborate complexity of each. Thought must bring such double increase of difficulty quickly to a halt, not only because of its being insupportable in itself but because the whole business of choice is necessarily subject to a deadline.

Besides the logical consequence of supposing choice to be effective, that is, originative, and not merely responsive, subservient, automatic and empty, there is another evident basic consideration bearing on the matter of horizon, namely, the human life-span. No doubt human beings are deeply concerned with the prospects of their more immediate descendants, but since each successive generation of conceivable descendants will owe a smaller and smaller fraction of its genetic inheritance to a particular ancestor, the notion of 'perpetuating the succession' is largely a matter of names. A man may reasonably wish to think of himself as being genetically represented in time-to-come, but his own choices can have little reach to that end beyond one or two generations.

Economists have habitually spoken of 'impatience'. A specific situation, or transformation of one situation into another, is thought to have less meaning and influence for an individual, to matter less to him, the more remote the time at which it is imagined to take place. The question what can explain or underly such 'impatience', if it has a genuine existence, is exceedingly subtle. Animal needs, such as hunger, bound up with survival, are imperious. All other success depends on their being met. Also success of those kinds which provide the means of further enterprise may be more efficacious and powerful in doing so if gained early rather than late. If money can be lent so as to accumulate at compound interest, a stated sum will rise to a greater amount by a particular date (the rate of interest being given) the earlier it is available to be lent. Thus the equivalent in spot cash, available 'now', of a named sum is smaller, the more remote the date when that sum is assumed to be received. Biological and institutional fact may thus explain some impatience. It is sometimes suggested that imagined enjoyments, takings-place imagined and thus 'enjoyed beforehand', by anticipation, are keener in their effect in 'the present' if their supposed date of occurrence is near rather than far. But why should this be so? All such *enjoyment by anticipation* is the fruit of imagination, not, directly, of reports from the field. All are located by the individual's thought in time-to-come. What relevance has the calendar-date of such location on the keenness or effectiveness of the anticipative experience? There is one consideration which seems plainly a valid ground for distinguishing the degrees of enjoyment (or distress) which are derivable from an experience of one and the same formal character, whose occurrence is imagined for a nearer or for a more remote date. It is the question of what, below, I shall call the *epistemic standing* of the supposition of this occurrence.

If the chooser deemed every rival supposition he could think of, which he might substitute for this one, to be fatally obstructed, so that this supposition, being the uniquely possible one, would have to be regarded as *certain*, that might be one extreme of the range of epistemic standing within which he must locate it. At the other extreme the supposition which he is concerned with might itself be fatally obstructed, and so be regarded as *impossible*. I shall adopt a different meaning for the range of epistemic standing, and regard it as extending, not from impossibility to certainty, but from impossibility to perfect possibility. Whichever of these two meanings we give to the notion of a range of epistemic standing, it seems plausible that the supposition of an occurrence of a given form, which is deemed 'highly possible' will have greater effect on the chooser's feelings and choice of action in his present, than one which is deemed 'nearly impossible'. If, then, such greater possibility seems to be conferred by a nearer location in time-to-come, we can say that there is in this conjuncture of ideas a possible source of 'impatience'. In more conventional terms, we should be ascribing impatience to 'uncertainty'.

In my theme, the skein of imagined sequels which the chooser conceives for any contemplated course of action will include sequels which are counter-desired, besides some which are desired. 'Impatience' seems applicable only to the sequels which are desired. However, the notion of horizon applies also to counter-desired sequels. If remoteness in time-to-come renders them more and more difficult to accept as possible, this will absolve the chooser's practical conscience from allowing them influence on his choice of action, when their main imagined effect lies far enough from his present.

The considerations which lead us to the notion of time-horizon carry us to a somewhat more general idea. Let us ask with what degree of detail and precision the chooser will describe to himself each imagined sequel of present action? The degree of such exactness, which is formally and logically conceivable, may well seem to constitute an infinite progression towards limitlessly finer *minutiae*. But in the practical business of choice, the chooser will deem the great mass of such minutiae as irrelevant. He is concerned with 'broad' effects. 'Success' and 'disaster' will in effect be *symbols*. Takings-place of various form and detailed content may equally represent for him the sign and assurance of success. A business man desires for his firm a large and rapid growth of business. The precise details of its evolution matter less than the brief summation given by an annual percentage increase. The statesman seeks to be remembered in history by great steps of attainment, but these will be things publicly statable rather than the intensities of effort and emotion upon which his career has been borne forward. The notion of 'imagined sequel' must, I think, be thought of as a symbol able to be realized and embodied in any of a variety of detailed forms. The idea of such symbolic representation of the imaginable sequels of choice is related in some degree to that of valuation, to which we shall refer in a later chapter. Ambitions must be given a form simple enough to be easily called up in thought, to retain an identity, to provide bearings in the making of choices under the pressure of a deadline. They must be encapsulated in a name, a place on a scale of desiredness (or, with haunting anxieties or counter-ambition, a place on the negative part of such a scale) or by a valuation in terms of other valuta.

)))
Epistemic possibility
(((

POSSIBILITY IS A judgement. It is a thought, but it is not entire knowledge. In the presence of entire knowledge a man would say, not that some taking-place imagined by himself was possible, but that it was the demonstrably unique truth-to-come. What is demonstrably the unique truth-to-come is evidently possible in a trivial sense. We are concerned with possibility adjudged to plural rivals. Possibility is relevant to choice when some imagined evolutions of affairs are judged to be *not* possible as sequels to some choosable course of action. If everything imaginable seemed a possible sequel of every choice, choice would be powerless and otiose. Choice is *effective* when it can confer or withhold possibility. It is effective, we may say, when there is a meaning for special, as well as general, possibility. Special possibility can, of course, lie only within general possibility.

Choice is effective if it can confer possibility. This sentence contains much of the essence of our theme. Its meaning and validity rest on our conception of the thinking being in his present and the confinement of his direct interest and concern to his thoughts. What he can do most immediately is to have thoughts, what his thoughts can do is to satisfy, by the resolves, the commitments, they contain and the sequels they accept as possible for those resolves, his need for imaginative repose, for having brought within imaginative reach the best attainable skein of rival *potentiae* of time-to-come.

Let us try to illuminate this picture more sharply by contrasting it with what he cannot do. He cannot lay his hands *directly* on

35

reports from the field to select and secure them. Reports from the field are beyond the reach of choice, they are not *possible*, they have occurred and are 'fact' in the literal sense, things that have been done. Possibility belongs to time-to-come, not to things the account of which occupies present thought. Does possibility then belong to Nature and to the field, or to the thinking being's thought? We have suggested that freedom of imagination supposes and rests on a freedom inherent in the field, an indeterminacy arising from the nature of choice itself as a *beginning*. The notion of choice as the originative fount of history, the notion of possibility as a conception standing over against determinism and unique certainty, are inseparably involved with each other and essentially bound up together. Let us insist on this meaning of possibility as a notion belonging indispensably to the notion of imaginative choice, of choice as a beginning, by calling it *epistemic possibility*. That is possible, which is not known by the individual chooser to be impossible, known in the sense of an answer given him when he appeals to his scheme or geometry of the field and his own supposition of his making a particular choice of action. For some specified evolution of affairs to be possible, in the sense relevant to the business of choice, requires a particular chooser with a particular scheme of the field.

Epistemic possibility is a judgement that some evolution of affairs in time-to-come is free of fatal obstacles discernible to the chooser. We might instead use the term *discerned* possibility, but this would suggest a claim that the way was *seen to be open* rather than that it was *not seen to be blocked*.

Epistemic possibility embraces three notions having more-special meanings. The widest of these, natural possibility, I shall use to refer to all states of the field, and transformations of such states, which do not seem to the chooser to be excluded by the principles of Nature or of human nature, the inherent fibre or constitution of the world. General possibility I have defined to mean the whole range of rival imaginable evolutions of affairs which seem to the chooser not to be precluded either by their lack

36

of natural possibility or by their requiring a starting-point which is not provided by the chooser's present. Special possibility will be adjudged by the chooser to a skein of rival histories-to-come which seem individually able to be realized on condition of his choosing a particular course of action. Special possibility is dependent on his choice. A different choice would withdraw special possibility from some imaginable histories-to-come and confer it on some which were excluded. In what sense, then, can we speak of such a skein, enjoying special possibility in view of a particular choice, being *bounded* in such a sense that a different choice would shift the bounds and bring into view a different skein?

A *course of action by the chooser* involves his dedication of particular resources, available to him in limited quantities, to specific kinds of use. Those whom he is able to employ must be given specified kinds of task, whose performance will preclude their performing other tasks. Physical materials which he can dispose of must be dedicated to some particular transformations, which will preclude their being devoted to other transformations. The tools and systems also whose employment he can control must be placed at the service of particular kinds of physical production. Action involves means, means are limited in quantity, capacity, power and reach, for any chooser. One pattern of their use will preclude other patterns. One such pattern will seem to confer special possibility on the imagined sequels composing one skein, a different pattern will confer it on those of a different skein. If there were no limitation of resources, in the ultimate sense of what a man can command either by present possession of it or by exchange of other possessions of his, the notion of choice would be empty. Choice would be unnecessary. The chooser could do and have everything on which the principles of Nature seem to confer natural possibility. But resources in any present *are* limited for human kind as a whole and for particular individuals. The need to choose is essential and fundamental in the human condition. Economics is the study of the business of choice. My theme

37

is the immeasurably more complex and subtle nature of that business than has been recognized by those versions of political economy which take their whole problem to be limitation of resources, and overlook the originative powers of thought involved and released in their use.

)))
Course of action, sequel of action
(((

IT WOULD BE a natural policy of thought to begin the study of
action by saying that this study is concerned with an evolution of
affairs in time-to-come, and that the field of study is this evolution
as a whole considered at first without regard to the question what
parts of it can be deemed to be actions of the chooser, and what
parts the sequel of those actions. For while the chooser is engaged
in the business of choosing, the time-to-come with which he is
concerned can for him be filled only with products of his own
thought. Whether a particular part of this work of origination, of
imagination, does or does not include deeds of his own as elements
in its pictures, all of it is in an essential sense figment. On what
ground, then, is it expedient or possible to divide any envisaged
course of history-to-come into *deed* and *sequel*? Although the
steps of action, the course of action, which he may choose will, at
the moment of choosing, be an imagined thing, such a step or
course, when chosen, will figure in his thought as something
unique, not a skein of rival entities. To *choose* is to commit oneself.
To choose is to eliminate what were, before the act of choice,
possible contents of time-to-come, but are now rejected. In order
to place himself in this position of being committed, the chooser
must have in view something which, in relation to what was open
before the act of choice, is a singled-out, unified and self-consistent
thing, not something comprising rivals in any relevant sense.
There will be severe constraints on the kinds, and calendar-
locations, of the takings-place which can be thus envisaged.
Beyond the bounds of such constraint, the singleness, the self-

consistency, will begin to dissolve. The notion of *commitment* will lose its force. The transition from that which can be resolved upon as a thing seen as unique, to that which comprises rival possibilities none of which can be excluded, will not be a sharp break, and will doubtless be difficult to locate precisely. This does not destroy its essential meaning and relevance. There are acts which seem plainly within the chooser's reach and capability, and there are the spreading, plural possibilities of what may flow from those acts. Action and sequel can be distinguished in essence, though this boundary may not be sharp and unambiguous.

Nonetheless, it seems plain that envisaged steps of action are symbols, the names of classes of exact notions, and not exact notions themselves. The man who bets on a particular racehorse in some race may never have seen a racehorse, may know nothing about the one which is to carry his money except its name and the names of its jockey, trainer and owner. The horse's name is a symbol, a *suggestion* of vaguely supposed things. Thus plurality springs directly and immediately from the seed of a definite act, though that act's definiteness, when it is envisaged beforehand, is itself the definiteness of a type of act. The place and time at which the punter will hand over his money, the person to whom he will hand it, may not be specified in his act of choice. The choice of action falls on a symbol of a class of actions. This need not destroy in any way the expediency of considering part of an imagined sequence of takings-place as action, part as sequel of action.

These ideas can be alternatively formulated by means of the word *policy*. This enables us to make explicit the evident truth that such part of the content of time-to-come which he may designate as an imagined *sequel* of an available course of action will itself include imagined acts of his own. The criterion which distinguishes course of action from sequel of action is the essential, irremediable plurality of the sequels assigned to (imagined for) any course, a plurality which flows from the nature of choice itself as we have elected to suppose it, the partly *ex nihilo* origination of contents for time-to-come. By contrast with the essential plurality of the sequels imagined for a course of action, the course itself, though composed of symbols (classes of precise acts) is a unique coherent whole not essentially involving mutual rivalry within its structure. The chooser may conceive the precise acts, by which his symbolic course could be embodied and realized, to be indifferent and equivalent amongst themselves, so that their plurality is of no significance.

Policy is a scheme of action, but it is not confined to the notion of a course of action in the sense of an essentially self-consistent and entirely unified conception. For policy serves well as the name for the chooser's conception of the part his own acts will play in any single imagined sequel of such a course. The acts of his own which he locates in remoter time-to-come cannot be free of mutual rivalry. Any such act, being part of one imagined sequel of a present act out of many sequels deemed possible, will depend for its realization on the realization of that part of this sequel which is located between the chooser's present and the calendar-date to which this act is assigned. The notion of policy directs attention to the need of the chooser to be ready to respond, in this way or that, to states of affairs which are mutually rival possibilities. Policy is thus a notion which embraces both of our divisions of imagined content of time-to-come, both that part which is deemed to be unequivocally within the chooser's capability and reach, and that part which consists of plural envisaged possibilities.

Let us remark that the notion of policy depends on that of the need and instinct to imagine time-to-come in many variants. The notion of policy is that of an attitude and underlying purpose or intended pursuit, whose embodiment in action will take this form or that according to the situation which may confront the chooser in time-to-come. Such a situation may prove to be one of those which he now envisages as a possible sequel of a chosen course. But the chooser may also have in mind the notion that his skein of imagined sequels for this course can prove not to have encompassed the history which will be reported. How far will it be consistent for him to make allowance and preparation for the insufficient inclusiveness of his skein of envisaged sequels?

I am supposing the skein of sequels imagined by the chooser for any specified course of action to be in principle unlimited in the plurality of its members, yet at any present moment in the chooser's business of choice, to be bounded in the sense that there is amongst the sequels which he has imagined up to that moment a most desired and a most counter-desired sequel. The sequels comprised in any skein are required to be possible in his judgement, that is, unobstructed by any fatal obstacle discernible to him. It is the requirement of adjudged possibility which will place bounds on any skein. The question is therefore a very subtle one, whether his recognition of the incompleteness (and even the uncompletability) of a skein as far as he has conceived it at any present moment, will be a ground for his questioning the ultimate validity of the bounds of the skein in terms of his valuation of its extreme members. However, it may be suggested that from the outset of his considering what sequels could flow from any specified available course of action, he will seek to set these bounds as far apart as he can, and thus to give them validity in both his immediate business of choosing amongst courses of action, and in a more fundamental view. In a subsequent chapter we shall consider how possibility can be represented by a *scale of feeling*. The appropriate particular feeling is that of (potential) surprise. Let us say, therefore, that at any stage of his construction of a skein of sequels, it will seem to him potentially somewhat surprising if a sequel yet to be thought of should prove to extend the bounds of the skein, yet not surprising to such a degree as to constitute a judgement that this is impossible. We shall discuss, below, the opening this consideration gives for considering *elasticities of surprise*.

The term policy in the sense which we are giving to it would serve as a summary account or name for what we have called the *rival choosables*. Choice of action, let us then say, is choice amongst *policies*. The notion of policy implies a general orientation of the chooser's taste or temperament towards a broad class of sequels.

His chosen action will be designed to give *special possibility* to a skein of imagined sequels which, taking together its desired and counter-desired members, gives him a better anticipative satisfaction than any other. But the possibility of any one of its rival member-sequels will depend on his supposing himself to perform in time-to-come some actions called for by, and helping to constitute, that sequel. Where such actions will be required is unknowable in advance. Thus a choice of policy means a preparedness to undertake this or that action according to the situation realized in time-to-come. It may be asked why, if a counter-desired sequel seems to depend for its realization on actions of his own, it should not be prevented from realization by omitting these actions. The answer is that to omit these actions would lead to a worse subsequent evolution of affairs than to perform them.

The notion of policy has, implicit within it, that of uncertainty, that is, plurality of envisaged possibilities. Policy is the pursuit of desired sequels in face of a recognition that their attainment can only be deemed possible at the cost of making also possible some counter-desired sequel.

)))
The incentive for choosing.
Choice as commitment
(((

W HAT DOES THE business of choosing do for the chooser? But
first, *when* does the business do something for the chooser? No
doubt purposeful thought is entertaining in itself, absorbing and
even exciting. But being purposeful, the chooser's business of
thought is not a mere pastime continuing aimlessly. It aims at a
conclusion, at a *state of things.* That state of things, to be known to
the chooser, must reside in his thought. It must be a state of his
thought. Thought, we have argued (though it needs no argument)
exists in the transient present or *is* the present. The business of
choosing has its effect in some present moment of the chooser's
thought.

It is not for the sake of some formal shape of thought that the
arduous business of choice would be undertaken. Emotion must
be involved. In order to experience emotion, the chooser must
involve *himself* in the state of things he contemplates, the state
which his act of choice is intended to produce. He must *commit*
himself. Choice is commitment. The state of things which choice
aims at is a state of feelings induced by what I ventured to call the
imagined, deemed possible. By a choice of action, a chooser gives a
significance, an orientation, to his resources of all kinds, a list that
includes above all his own gifts of the psyche, his capacities for
thought, for the intuitive touching of the keyboard of another's
imagination, for influencing or impelling others; his material
possessions, considered in their technical design and powers; the
entire range of persons whom he can induce to act in ways which
he can symbolize to himself. This dedication of resources to a line

44

of action or a skein of endeavours, exposes him to possibilities which otherwise would have been excluded: nothing venture, nothing win. But venture means also exposure to possibilities of misfortune or disaster, which also might have been excluded by a different choice. The imagined, rendered possible, is the generative focus of the enjoyment and satisfaction afforded by choice, an enjoyment by *anticipation*, by imagination. What, then, does choice do for the chooser? It puts within reach a good state of mind. Can choice secure desired reports from the field? Not within what we must call the transience between two transients, not in the immediate, emergent moment of time-to-come. What is within reach is not the desired reports themselves, which if they ever come, will do so only after a lapse of time; it is the imagination of those desired reports as *possible*. Choice is commitment that renders a desired sequel possible.

But what, then, is commitment? It is the chooser's staking of his moral consistency and self esteem. To abandon choice once made, save for *force majeure*, is to suffer a psychic injury. If the chooser does not *commit* his means of action, possibility of imagined sequels is impaired, for short of commitment to one course of action, another might replace it, with the consequence of obstructing the sequels imagined for the former course. Possibility depends on commitment, and anticipative satisfaction depends on possibility of imagined sequels.

A *good state of mind* has both its formal and its emotional basis and essential nature. Thoughts have form, but that form touches the chooser's *potentiae* of joy and sorrow. How can the purely formal, the contemplation of a purely abstract, linguistic or symbolic statement, affect the feelings which engender action? What is the link of an abstraction and the emotional currents which sweep men along? It is the link supplied by *choice*. Choice is the staking of a man's effort, resources and hopes on a course of action, symbolically but effectively outlined, which exposes him to a more intense level of imaginative experience than that of mere 'geometry'. He has by a *choice* embarked his thought upon a tide. To abandon that voyage will be, in some degree, a self-betrayal. Choice is exposure to possibilities, and possibilities are those imagined sequels of particular commitment which have presented themselves to the chooser and eluded the objections and obstructions which his knowledge, that is, his Scheme and his awareness of his visible circumstances in the present, can show him. Throughout its argument, my theme is an appeal to various molecular unities of ideas. Choice is the *evolution* of a state of mind, from contemplation of the abstract and formal, to recognition of emotions within reach, attainable by means of these formal conceptions but not yet seized, to election and seizure of their actuality by commitment. Choice is the origination of forms; the rejection of some by the denial to them of natural, general or special possibility; the giving of special possibility and thereby emotional force to some by the moral act of commitment. Choice is the transition from *dunamis* to *entelechy*, but this entelechy, this actuality of being, is an actuality of emotional imagination.

We speak of moments of time, but each present exists, takes place, only in its very transformation into its merging successor. The paradox which baffles verbalization is the unity and identity of two discernible aspects, the individual moment and that moment's essence of continuous vanishing into another moment. The notion of 'the present' is that of an entity whose being is a ceasing to be itself and is a transformation into a different entity. The aspect of 'the present' which we can seek to point to by such expressions as *transience, unity of coming and going, continuous evolution*, can also be seen as a paradoxical simultaneity of successive phases. Each present is a complex of images of shading degrees of immediacy and of sharp completeness or embryonic vagueness, each present reaches out by imagination to the phases which will carry it into its successor. The two aspects, distinct in formal conception but identical in essence, confront us with something reminiscent of the paradox of the arrow. The arrow at each instant stands at a point of space and of time, yet the arrow has as the *potentiae* of its present state, the points of space and of time-to-

46

come whose conjuncture constitutes its movement. We can think of the arrow either as *being in motion at one place*, or as *standing* at *successive instants and places*. The present consists partly in the imaginative inclusion of its succession of phase-sequels of receding degrees of immediacy. Does 'the present' move into time-to-come or does it encompass a certain depth of graded and softening immediacy? Either image may serve for some attempts at intellection or expression; one may be on some occasions more suggestive than the other. Time-present, time-to-come, are not divided by a boundary but are continuously involved one in the other and born of each other, the very being of time-present consists in its imaginative engendering of merging phases which carry it into its successor.

Language is, of course, incapable of more than a fumbling suggestion of the enigma. For my theme, the need to attempt some verbal symbolism, however alien to our direct intuitions it may seem, arises from the domination of our time-ideas by an artefact, the notion of time as extension, as a space in the abstract sense. For we have been led to speak of 'the future', that is, of 'what is to be', as though this was the furniture of another room in our house, existing now but not visible until we move there. Thought which is the present; the present which spans the News and the Imagined, deemed Possible, attaining *in the present* the results of choice, not as News, not as reports from the field, but as a present good state of mind, a good state of imagination; choice which finds its incentive and its reward in an *immediacy* which fuses the present and the edge of time-to-come; an immediacy where imagination can perceive an attainable state of thought and realize it as an attained satisfaction: this is our conception of thought, time and choice, the ever-transient, present, sole existent.

)))
Beginning: *cause uncaused*
(((

CAUSE IN ONE sense is the notion of a subsequent governed in form and nature by an antecedent. If that governance is deemed entire, nothing, in the taking-place of this subsequent, has begun. The subsequent, if observed as a taking-place, is the mere revelation of something already existent, the more extended revelation of the essential nature of the antecedent. If cause in this sense were universal, encompassing all takings-place including thought, there would be no place in the scheme of things for *beginnings*.

Beginning I use here as the term for a taking-place in which some element, aspect or character is *ex nihilo*. No knowledge of antecedents, however complete and exact, would make possible a foreknowledge of that aspect or character. The word is intended to convey a further suggestion: that if the taking-place in question had been different, in the respect in which it is *ex nihilo*, the sequel would have been different. In the sense with which I wish to invest this word, beginning is a cause, itself in some respect uncaused. Such a conception raises questions concerning the notion of cause itself, which must be touched on. If cause, in the sense of governance of subsequents by antecedents, were all-pervasive and all-encompassing, the world so characterized would be a determinist world in whose history time would be a mere canvas allowing the relative location of particulars. Takings-place, foreordained to the last detail, would be the mere sequential revelation, to an illuded human consciousness, of the items of a picture eternally complete. How, in such a picture, or to what purpose and effect, could 'the cause' of any item be identified? The picture as a whole

48

would be the only thing to which its parts or items could be ascribed by way of explaining them. In these considerations there appears a powerful suggestion, powerful both in capacity for conviction and in consequence: *Cause* requires the notion of *beginning*.

In an all-embracing structure whose parts or particulars are united in a universal interlocking of their natures, causal chains are not meaningfully discernible. If what exists in one place in the eternal picture is the only thing that could exist there, we cannot speak of cause. We can speak of cause only if something that takes place can be conceived, imagined, to have been different from what it is. To cause is to make a difference. To say that some taking-place could have been different is to invoke the notion of *ex nihilo*, of non-governance, of uncause. Either this taking-place, which we claim could have been different, is itself a beginning in our sense, or it has received an essential impulse from such a beginning. If choice is the locus of beginning, we must say that *choice* is necessary to *cause*.

The notion of cause is necessary to a meaningful notion of choice, and that of choice is necessary to a meaningful notion of cause. The effective idea is a unified one. Unless the unity and inter-active fibre of the field is subject to incisions, to breaks, there can be no distinguishing one thread of this fibre from another as a particular 'cause' of some other thread or item. But if there are takings-place which could have been different even within the same tissue of other takings-place that actually prevailed; could have been different, that is to say, despite natural principles and 'laws'; then such a *beginning* can be, in the utmost and extreme meaning of the word, an *origin*, a source beyond which there is no discerning any governing or generative circumstance; a source beyond which it is otiose to search for explanation. From such a beginning, ripples and pulses of consequential effect will flow according to natural laws. Some takings-place will be traceable to that beginning, and it will be meaningful to say that if that beginning had been different (as it could have been, within the same texture of other history) then these subsequent takings-place would have been different. The *beginning* has had a causal influence on their character.

The core of my theme is to be found in this molecular pattern of words: *uncause*, freedom of a thought to be one thing or another or another – within a given texture of impressions from the field and of antecedent thoughts; *beginning*, the power of such a thought to induce a sequel different from those of other thoughts which could have occurred in place of it; *cause*, the governance of a subsequent by antecedents according to the principles of Nature and of suggestion affecting thoughts. There is a seeming paradox. Without uncause there can be no freedom; without freedom there can be no beginning; without beginning there can be no cause; without cause there can be no effectiveness of choice. The unity of the idea thus sought to be described is in danger of being obscured by the need for a triad of words to describe it. Its import will not be readily accepted. The whole current of modern thought is to look behind every report from the field, every taking-place, every observation, for something else which can be held indispensable to this report or taking-place. That something else, in turn, must have its 'explanation', its determining circumstances. Thus there builds itself up a complete fabric of inter-locking necessities; what happened in any part of the scene is the only thing that could happen there. Where, then, is choice? Or should we ask, What is choice? in the world of the infinite regress of analysis and complete explanation, except the mere bolting-together of the parts of the structure, with bolts of pre-determined form? The notion of uncause may be alien to the modern scientific ethic (though 'randomness' is invoked in the mechanism of evolution; the heritable 'chance' mutation, it seems, is not yet deemed explicable) but if we bind ourselves into this structure we must mean by choice mere determinate response, the inter-action of the cogs of the machine. Men cannot then suppose themselves the makers of history. Will you have universal cause, or will you have originative choice? *Beginning, uncause*, is necessary to cause, unless cause means rigid, eternal determinate history.

My theme has a formal structure somewhat distinct from the texture of the human scene and business which I seek to illuminate by its means. That business centres for us on the term *choice*. I have sought to justify the rejection of one received notion of choice, namely, that of the empty and determinate upshot of a confrontation of the individual's endowment of tastes and his historically given and in some way fully known circumstances. We have asked what ought here to be meant by 'circumstances', and have answered that in relation to present choice of action they ought to include everything which in time-to-come can shape the sequel of that present choice. Amongst these shaping influences will be the choices to be made in time-to-come. Can the character of those be known in the present? Not if *choice* is deemed to illustrate in the scene of human business (human activity of any sort) the abstract and formal notion of *beginning* which I have sought to define. The nature of *beginning* ensures in a complex mode the inviolable blankness of time-to-come in matters where humans are involved. For we are supposing that time-to-come is void in those matters until beginnings have played a part in filling it. But if beginnings are thoughts partly *ex nihilo*, the character and the calendar occurrence of beginnings in time-to-come can neither be seen by the eye-witness in the present nor inferred from their antecedents in the present. If choices are beginnings, they can be the originators, not merely the carriers of history.

In proposing a theme which collides with some of the essential if often tacit and even unconscious assumptions of historians as well as natural scientists, I feel obliged to be wholly uncompromising in statement but also to show with the utmost care what are those internal contradictions of orthodoxy which seem to demand a radical resolution. What are the aims of the historiographer? He sometimes declares his aim to be merely 'to tell what happened'. Yet if 'what happened' refers merely to the publicly visible acts of selected people, what constitutes an act? Can it be described in purely physical terms? It seems obvious that history in terms of purely physical description would be worthless and intolerable. An act is surely something purposeful. Yet to assign or suggest purpose is to *explain*. History becomes teleology. Already then, it is at odds with determinism. For in a determinist world there can be no role for purpose except an illusory and passive one. In a determinist world, what room is there for explanation of any kind, except the simple statement, 'This is how things were from eternity designed to be'. History seems, of its essential nature, to involve purpose. But is not purpose the character of an act which might have been rejected in favour of a different act? If I am led by the desire to effect some purpose, to act in a particular way, the implication is that I could have acted in a different way. Purpose involves choice, and choice implies plural possible courses, and this plurality itself, affecting everyone, implies unknowledge of the outcome of any choice. The kind of historiography which all of us seek is the kind which attributes acts to the thoughts of men, which supposes those thoughts to be not wholly analysable into ante- cedent circumstances of a kind which in principle would be publicly visible, and thus sees in men's thoughts a *ne plus ultra* of explanation. The question is, if we retreat at all from this position, can we stop anywhere short of determinism? Law, politics, historiography, commerce, are described by their practitioners in terms which implicitly suppose there are beginnings in our sense, choices in our sense. What sense would the proceedings of these practitioners make, what depths of illusion would they not imply, if we denied all validity to such a notion as ours of *beginning*?

The account men give themselves of their affairs seems at first sight full of paradox. They see in them a teleological meaning, the flowing consequence of endeavours of individuals each seeking to realize an imagined end or continuing purpose, endeavours which nonetheless affect, divert, condition and partly frustrate each other, endeavours which express choices amongst rival courses within reach, those choices being in some essential sense their chooser's own original, ungoverned novelties of imagination, using sug- gestions from the News and the Scheme, but injecting, in some respect *ex nihilo*, the unforeknowable arrangement of elements. Do men, then, choose their own history? Plainly no man can do so, since by the nature of non-illusory choice he cannot know what will be the sequel of any act of his. Yet if choice is non-illusory, history is created by men's choices. Choices are elections of ends or purposes, they are assignments of epistemic possibility to some kinds or degrees of realization of those ends, they rely on applications of reason to some scheme of the nature of the field including the other persons who compose it, yet reason must work with material which is not given and known circumstance but imagined and supposed circumstance. The historiographer can without presumption or absurdity trace that reason as he conceives it to have been applied to those suppositious data which he himself, detached and speculative observer, supposes men to have supplied themselves with. Must not 'explanation in history' have a texture of this kind? It cannot pretend to say how it came about that men chose this or that action, for such choices, according to the theme we are pursuing, are essentially unaccountable beginnings. In order to give his art a shaping spirit or meaning, the historian is irresistibly driven to explain. But the nature of his explanation shares all the uncertainty, the unknowledge in vital respects, of the stream of transformations which are its subject-matter.

)))
Beginning and Unforeknowledge
(((

THE THEME PURSUED in these pages can be seen from different standpoints as different molecular combinations of ideas. One such embraces the notions of origination and unforeknowledge. Our language has no word whose meaning is purely that of divorce from antecedents. The word origin itself may convey the notion of a particular setting of circumstance, and operation of principle, which by their nature give rise to a taking-place, or an entity, of determinate form deducible from those antecedents. It is because of this that I have sought to adopt the word *beginning*, in a sense rather like that of the first sentence of King James's bible, to mean a taking-place or an entity which in some respects owes nothing to the past. What is thus uninherited may be only an arrangement of elements whose individual forms, though abstract and merely typical, are familiar. The resolution of any present scene, which occupies the individual's thought, into elements and their arrangement may seem arbitrary. The purpose served by using two such terms can be suggested rather than defined. A musical composition uses notes which are like those played countless times before, yet the composition itself has not before been singled out from the more-than-infinitely* many possible patterns of such notes as a thing in itself.

There can be no eye-witnessing of the content of time-to-come. If there is to be foreknowledge of it, in any sense, that must depend on recognizing the antecedents of that content and ascribing to them the power to determine it. *Beginning* is an assertion that such

* Infinities of higher cardinalities have their place in our theme.

power may be sometimes absent. In finding a locus for *beginnings* in some kinds of thought, we are proposing to treat these kinds of thought as exempt from determinism and thus from foreknowledge. If there are *beginnings*, there is no complete inferential knowledge of the content of time-to-come. If there is also no eye-witness knowledge of it (to suppose such would be a contradiction in terms) there is no foreknowledge which can claim to be certain and complete. But we must also look at this argument from the other end. If choice is to mean something other than obedience to the dictates of visible circumstance confronting given tastes, its freedom, its capacity to go beyond such dictates, must consist in its identity with the notion of beginning as we are seeking to use it.

I feel it needful to insist on and re-iterate these considerations, for they are alien not only to Laplace's conception of the physical universe and his explicit inclusion in it of human affairs, but also to the modern economist's procedures in explaining the nature of 'business' and much of human activity. Either history is determinate and exists and reveals itself on its own and makes use of the passive subservience of men while allowing to 'choice' no meaning but that of mechanical linkage between earlier and later states. Or else history is continually originated in each present, and history-to-come exists only in men's imaginative creation of it in many rival variants which will contend and inter-lace with each other to form each successive 'present'. Shall we opt for history which in principle is completely analysable and fully explicable, or for history ever in process of being *originated* in the extreme sense?

The upshot of these considerations is the inseparable unity of the notion of unforeknowledge with that of originative, that is, non-empty choice. Choice if it is effective on its own entails unknowledge of time-to-come. Non-empty choices will be made in that time, and will affect the sequel of present choice. The word decision, an alternative to choice, well serves the purpose of suggesting that originative perpetual creation of history by the pursuit of works of imagination into the sphere of action is a cutting into the fabric of governance of time-to-come by time past and thus a cutting of the deductive process based on knowledge of what has been the case. Decision means literally a cut. We may regard this as a cut between 'past and future', or as a cutting-off from the whole compass of the imagined, deemed possible, a skein of special possibilities depending on a particular commitment to action. In either view we conceive time-to-come as the void needing to be filled by work of imagination using suggested elements but not bound as to their arrangement. We have tried also to insist on the nature of the notion of elements as effectively an infinite regress, a process of perhaps endless resolution, into more and more primitive ideas, of the scene, the field or the Scheme. It may have been noticed that in the statement of my theme I have sought to avoid the word 'future'. 'Future' means something which 'is to be'. But we are here saying that there is no general evolution of human affairs which 'is to be'. The two views, of a future which pre-exists human cognisance and merely waits to be discovered, and which by greater skill and assiduity could be *discovered before its time*, and the view that the content of time-to-come is in some respects the product of present *beginning*, of origination involving something *ex nihilo*, are essentially and fundamentally in conflict. It has not seemed to me that this conflict is recognized or acknowledged by those who seek to 'analyse choice', that is, to explain that choice is not the essentially original creative act that our intuition may suggest, but the inevitable consequence of antecedents. Do we choose or do we merely reflect the operation of unarguable forces?

We have presented the supposition of determinism and that of continually originated history as rival policies of thought. In electing origination of history by choices which are beginnings in my sense, am I declaring that human conduct dispenses with reason? Every hour and every moment provides evidence that we pursue reason with unflagging ardour and indefeasible instinct and intuition. The imagined sequels and their claim to possibility must consult reason at every step; every constructed ambition must use reason as the indispensable sanction and the condition imposed by practical conscience. Reason, however, is the fitting together of ideas. The strong temptation of a theory of determinate conduct is to suppose, without argument, that the ideas which reason fits together are in some way *given*. Conduct, this view assumes, is the fitting together of a jigsaw puzzle. The pattern in which this can be done is unique, determined by the shapes of the pieces. Not only the need for the pieces to fit together, namely, the operation of reason, but also, in the determinist view, the pieces themselves are given. We have elected, by contrast, to suppose that the shapes of the pieces are originated by the chooser. When the chooser has imagined them, reason still dictates that they be fitted together. Non-determinism is as much the employer of reason as determinism. It recognizes, however, the question: Whence are the ideas that we reason about?

The notion of beginning and the notion of unforeknowledge are inseparable strands in a thread of thought. But time-to-come must, by the compulsion of human instinct and practical conscience, be somehow filled, in the present. If only one evolution of affairs in that time could be seen by any chooser as unobstructed, in his knowledge, he would have to treat that one evolution as uniquely certain. The recognition of unknowledge is the recognition of plural possibilities. This plurality has essential implications for our search for a language in which to describe and explain men's business of choice.

It is doubtless from the Greeks that we have inherited our confidence in the reach and power of human thought. They did not acknowledge that any aspect of the universe was beyond them. In the latest centuries science has taken up this outlook and its implication, that men can know whatever, with sufficient ardour and sustained effort, they seek to know. Does this posture of mind amount to a denial of the ultimate reality of an unforeknowable time-to-come? Many public pronouncements, much of the practice and the language of business and politics (those two aspects of one essentially unified acquisitive activity) suggest that unforeknowledge is an idea scarcely able to be assimilated into the foundations of modern conduct. In the thought-practice of those who conduct our affairs, unforeknowledge is treated as alien, intolerable, unbelievable. There *must* (so it would seem from the public face of politics and business) be a method and a means of foreknowledge. Military aggressions on a vast scale, unthinkably evil in aim and method, have been based on the supposition that *calculation* can tell men what action will produce what effect. It seems that men do not ask themselves why one side in a headlong conflict, a conflict from which all compromise or concession is necessarily excluded, should have an access to infallible foreknowledge which by its meaning must deny such foreknowledge to the other side.

The procedure of calculation by which, in such attitudes, it is proposed to ignore, deny and sweep aside the enigma of the source of history, is some form of calculus of probability. We do not know uniquely and for certain (these calculators seem to say) what will be the outcome of this démarche or that? Very well, we can assign to various outcomes numerical values which express their respective 'probabilities'? What, in this context, does this word mean? Men who are proposing to overturn the lives and history of great populations seem to treat this intention as though it were a *divisible experiment*, a series of many trials all made under conditions stable in some respects, and all *contributing* to a total result which was what mattered to the calculators. A course of action which by its evident and unmistakable nature and purpose declares itself to be a *crucial*, indeed a *self-destroying*, experiment, an inherently and essentially once-for-all, all-or-nothing throw of the die, is treated as though it could be repeated again and again in the building up of a result.

If choice is non-illusory, non-empty, non-powerless, choice is the imaginative filling of a void. The very nature of such choice implies the meaninglessness of 'foreknowledge'. How can choice be based on foreknowledge of what that choice is called on to create? The imagined histories-to-come to which a particular resolve, a particular commitment, gives special possibility, are mutually exclusive *rivals*. What has the language of mathematical expectation to do with such thoughts?

The assumption that 'probability', in some sense which can yield a numerical basis for calculation, can turn essential unknowledge into knowledge, is inherently self-contradictory. Are we saying that experience counts for nothing? Of course we are not propounding a nonsense so monumental and all-embracingly absurd. Experience, the record and the memory of reports from the field, is the source of suggestion, the fuel of imagination though not its determinate governance. The building-blocks of the Scheme, the language of the News, the tesserae of the rival mosaics of history-to-come, are supplied by interpreted and stored impressions, by 'experience'. Experience *suggests what can* come to pass. If experience could tell us what *will* come to pass, we should be in a world of determinate history, choice-denying and choice-abolishing.

A question which the student of human affairs cannot avoid is the relation between the origination of the content of time-to-come and the explanation of the content of time past. If time-to-come is the unforeknowable void, what can the historiographer say of the meaning of what the traces and the records tell him of time past? Our theme takes a distinct view of the nature of history, of what it is that men's consciousness and the reports from the field tell them about. We are supposing that history exists only in taking place, that its course is constrained by in some sense *ex nihilo* creation going on from one 'present moment' to another. The creative process, we are supposing, takes place by means of the human imagination, using building-blocks whose character also is shaped by imagination from suggestions supplied by reports from the field. The field thus influences in two ways the course that history takes, giving it a continuity of a particular kind, but leaving it undetermined within the constraints of the material situation which its past course has brought into being in 'the present' and the suggestions out of which imagination improvises its skeins of possibilities for time-to-come. Then, is that *continuity* such that the historiographer can claim, in some interesting or useful sense, to 'explain' the past evolution of human affairs which he discerns in the testimony (of artefacts and documents) offered to his eyes by the present?

The historiographer knows of men's driving instincts and types of ambition. There is the universal instinct of survival and the guarding of successors; the desire for acquisition and wealth for the sake of the 'consequence' or the influence that they confer, or the evidence they show of personal capacities and prowess; the wish to out-rival others in some art or exercise; the wish for fame; the wish for authority, for not ignoble reasons; and the base urge for power; there is the wish to create beauty; the hope of achieving sanctity. If these are men's ends, the historiographer can seek in the record for signs of their pursuit. He may ask himself, concerning particular moves, what knowledge and what insights composed the Scheme of the individual concerned at the time when his action was chosen, and what sort of hopes and fears this picture of encompassing circumstance would have allowed or compelled him to entertain. The business of choice, I am maintaining, is the business of imagination. The business of historiography, therefore, is the effort to penetrate one man's imagination by another's. Evidently, such art of historiography will be precarious and unsure, it will be 'poetry'. The Greeks believed it was the poet who could get nearest to the truth.

)))

*Desiredness, boundedness, and unidependence of
rival imagined sequels of choice*

(((

In the theme I am proposing, choice rests ultimately on the
entities which I have called imagined paths of history-to-come. I
suppose choice to determine in some way which of such paths are
to serve as the basis of the chooser's good state of mind, his commitment to a course of action and his contentment to rest his hopes
upon it, despite the compulsion of practical conscience to accept
both desired and counter-desired imagined sequels of the action
as possible. I deem each course of action within the chooser's
reach to have its skein of such imagined sequels, distinct in some
respects from that of other available actions. A different choice of
action would bring into operation a different skein. Within each
skein the imagined sequels are mutual rivals. The questions ought
therefore to be explicitly asked and answered: What is meant
when we say that a different choice of action shifts the chooser's
anticipative basis of feeling to a different skein? How does it come
about that sequels which are rivals and mutually exclusive are
bound into one skein, while others are excluded from this skein
and bound into other skeins? Can we speak of the *bounds* of such a
skein, and what will this term mean?

A path of history must evidently be conceived as a locus of
points in a space of as many dimensions as there are, in the chooser's
thought, different characters, qualities or measurable features of a
historic situation. A situation of affairs can be thought of as a
vector of as many elements as needed for effective description.
These elements will comprise all the public statistics and private
book-keeping quantities which interest the chooser, conceived of

course as belonging to time-to-come. Each such vector can be represented in thought as a point in a many-dimensioned space. Then a path of history will be a series of such points taken in time-sequence. In what sense can so complex a conception be thought of as serving as a boundary of a skein of such paths?

It is evident that we do not require such a boundary to consist of the extreme values in every dimension, which are to be found amongst the entire skein, on that side where paths are 'desired' or on the side of the skein where paths are 'counter-desired'. There may be no path which consists of all such extreme values. The concept of a boundary must refer to the notion of the *desiredness* of some one path (on the desired or on the counter-desired side) considered as a whole.

Moralists and economists have long since abjured any concern with the basis of taste. A path of history-to-come, which the chooser imagines and deems to be a possible sequel of a specific course of action within his reach, must be supposed to be assessed by him as the painter assesses a landscape or as a viewer assesses a painting; as a critic assesses any work of art or as any sensual being derives enjoyment or its opposite from a complex of qualities of some unified entity, object or situation. A musical composition is a thing of very great complexity and subtlety, yet a hearer may be in various distinct degrees moved to enchantment or more muted pleasure by it. We need not feel obliged to explain how the chooser assigns to any imagined path of history a location, absolute or relative, on a scale or 'space' of desiredness. One path of history-to-come is 'good' and is better than another. One path is bad and is worse than another. The bounds of a skein of sequels must be the most desired and the most counter-desired of the sequels belonging to the skein. What, then, binds rival sequels into one skein?

What so binds them is evidently that the sequels of one skein are rival answers to one and the same question: What will follow if I take this course? A course of action, however, will be specified in terms of particular resources or means which are to be committed, and we can say that rival imagined sequels of a course of action are bound into one skein by their being the supposed fruit of the same set of resources. For the business-man, the typical 'course of action' which looks to a stretch of years to come is investment in a system of productive equipment. The exploitation of that system, when it has been created, will be able to take many alternative forms, each able, so far as the investing business-man can tell when he decides upon his investment, to have any one of a wide range of degrees of failure or success. In any such case, the skein of rival sequels is a skein of rival answers to a question concerning particular initial use of particular resources or means. The question and the resource or assemblage of means concerned are what unify the skein.

In saying that the boundedness of a skein of sequels must refer to the chooser's assignment, to its member-sequels, of degrees, or at least a comparison, of desiredness or counter-desiredness, we are saying that boundedness requires him to *value* the sequels. Valuation is a judgement or aesthetic response influenced by perhaps a great number and variety of characters or measures which the chooser discerns in a particular imagined sequel. The need for such a thought-process, the process of valuation, is inescapable. There is no 'objective', publicly visible or publicly valid basis for assigning degrees of relative importance to various characters or features of an imagined history-to-come. Their effect on the chooser depends as much on his own nature as on that of the history itself. Valuations are made by individuals. If, in the market-place, they are brought to co-incidence or to a point where exchange takes place, this is achieved by a choice of appropriate conduct on the part of the exchangers. As the economists say, effective valuation is 'at the margin', and the position of the margin can be varied by varying the quantities exchanged. Valuation is not ignoble, it is a part of the technical art of survival and enjoyment.

It is the complex entity, an 'entire' skein of sequels of present contemplated action, when each such sequel is accorded possibility, that can be valued with logical consistency, in so far as the word

63

'entire' can here be given some practical if not absolute meaning. For if, by contrast, we consider the task of valuing a 'single object', a single situation or the contents imagined for some epoch or brief span of time-to-come, or some transformation of one such situation into another, we confront an unsolvable problem. The value which such an object, situation or taking-place will have for the chooser 'now', will depend on the circumstances which he supposes to precede, surround and follow that small particle, so to call it, of history-to-come. At what price, he must ask himself, will others be valuing that object or that taking-place at the epoch in question? Do not his conjectures or suppositions concerning their valuations-to-come have a bearing on the chooser's present valuation? In the language of political economy, we can say that *all markets*, save those for ephemeral goods of instant consumption, are *speculative*. All prices, that might be proposed to be paid to-day for any object or performance located in time-to-come, are subject to the chooser's unknowledge of time-to-come. Nothing can be valued, save on some assumptions as to the circumstances which will prevail when it will present itself and be available. But it is just such assumptions which are provided, in variety and mutual rivalry, by the chooser's skein of imagined possible sequels of a present choice. The mutual rivalry, the mutual exclusiveness, of the member-sequels of the skein is the manifestation or embodiment of the chooser's inescapable unknowledge of time-to-come. If the mutually rival sequels of the mutually rival skeins can be so exploited by him as to derive from them a 'good state of mind', they can be so exploited as to provide a background for valuing single items or incidents of imagined history-to-come. The value to the chooser of any such item or incident will spring from its *potentiae* for him, the way it can serve him in his capacity of an *exploiter of practically guided imagination* in pursuit of a good state of mind. By contrast with values assigned by such private and encompassing orientation, the prices adopted on a market for the sake of exchange are conventions. They are convenient working agreements which enable the business of life to be carried on. The market (even the 'futures' market) knows at most only a fraction of the circumstances of time-to-come. It counts on the fulfilment of contracts, its individual members stake their self-esteem on the making-good their private resolutions and commitments, but contracts and intentions cover only a little of the open questions of time-to-come even in its nearest stretches. The market's near-miracle of engendering apparently unanimously agreed prices shows unknowledge over-ridden and trampled down by the sheer necessity of getting on with the business of living.

Investment is the economist's name for the most far-reaching and psychically demanding of the business-man's characteristic, professional, activities. The demands it makes require the truly roundedly equipped and gifted business-man to have a remarkable outfit of intellectual, emotional, moral and above all 'poetic' characters and qualities. What he needs of the poet's psychic endowment is imagination. For the business of investment is the business of giving to an assemblage of resources now within his reach, a meaning based wholly on that complex fabric of thought which we have called the Imagined, deemed Possible, the variant rival paths of evolution of affairs which practical conscience allows him to envisage for some one *enterprise*, some one coherent, encompassing present lining-up of the component items of the assemblage. The term *an enterprise* can serve well as the name of what binds rival imagined sequels of a choice of action into one skein. The enterprise is the embodiment and the expression of a complex idea: the idea of directing certain resources into immediate forms and employments as a means of discarding in one move some of both the obstacles and the defences of the imaginative mind, allowing it to entertain hopes on condition of accepting anxieties. The forms and embodiments which the resources are given and the systems which are designed and built from them compose what we may call an *enterprise-investment*.

Let us describe one more of those close interlacements or mutual involvements of ideas, which we have several times proposed as a means of epitomizing a somewhat demanding theme. The ideas which have come together in this chapter are those of the unity-in-rivalry of a skein of imagined sequels of a specified course of action; the *special possibility* conferred on the members of this skein by the supposition that this course will be the chooser's elected action; the interpretation of 'course of action' as a distinct *orientation* of a particular list of resources, and the recognition of this list as the source of the unity of the skein; the adoption, for any such *action in pursuit of imagination* of the term *enterprise*, and for its technological and physical embodiment, whether as act or as result, of *enterprise-investment*.

)))
Epistemic standing,
its assessment and expression
(((

IF THE EVIDENCE on some question is taken to be relevantly complete, to include everything that bears on the matter; and if the logical inference from this evidence is that a particular answer to the question is the only one to which no fatal obstacle can be discerned; then, in relation to that evidence and its acceptance as containing the entire context of the matter, this answer is *certain*. In any other state of thought on the question, what can be said about any answers that are proposed? 'Other states of thought' fall into two classes. In one, the individual accepts that there can be in the nature of things no such thing as a body of evidence complete in the sense that all answers except one are excluded by it. In the other, he accepts that the evidence he possesses logically allows of more than one answer. In the first class of cases, there is a barrier beyond which it is meaningless to seek to probe with the purpose of distinguishing amongst suggested answers on grounds of their capacity to be realized as true. In the second class of cases, however, the individual may, without logical inconsistency, propose to himself a filling of any definable gaps in the evidence he possesses. According to the particular way in which he may suppose such a gap to be filled, one proposed answer or another may then be the logical consequence of the imaginatively augmented (completed) evidence. If, in some sense, it appears 'easier' to fill such a gap in one way rather than another, the standing accorded to one proposed answer may be superior to that of another. Evidently the effectiveness or applicability, the essential content of meaning, ascribable to this line of thought depends on our being able to give some content to the terms 'easier to imagine', 'easier to suppose', and to the term *standing*.

We may give to the term *epistemic standing* a formal meaning as follows. When all answers except one to some question appear to be excluded by the evidence, and that evidence is regarded as finally complete and impregnable, then that unique answer is taken to be *certain*. If there are discerned fatal objections to some answer, that answer is *excluded*. If, in some manner, it can be said that a particular answer is not certain and is not excluded, then we may consider whether its standing, which in other circumstances would be that of certainty or exclusion, can be treated as the occupancy of an interval between certainty and exclusion. On general grounds we might expect to be able to give various meanings or essential natures to such an interval, to stipulate for each such interpretation a test which would allow some suggested answer to some question to occupy that interval or would deny it entry; or in another view, a test which would itself confer operational meaning on that concept of the interval. Respecting any such interval, it seems that a suggested answer (hypothesis, proposition) might either claim mere occupancy, or that it might be assigned some location within the interval. If we claim to be able to assign *location* within the interval, we have to say precisely how this is to be adjudged, what is its meaning, and what use can be made of it.

The term *epistemic interval* is a mere vehicle for questions and possibilities. We have defined certainty of the validity of some hypothesis as involving both of two notions, the freedom of this hypothesis from obstruction, and the fatal obstruction of all rival hypotheses, whether they have been given explicit form or not. The presence, in the individual's thought, of plural hypotheses not fatally obstructed destroys certainty. Can we, however, speak either of the degree to which *certainty* of some hypothesis is *impaired* by the presence of rivals, or of the degree to which any hypothesis, considered on its own, is *obstructed*? Each of these two questions offers a meaning for the notion of an interval between

68

certainty and exclusion, within which comparisons of *standing* amongst hypotheses would be possible, and, perhaps, even their allocation to places on a scale of standing. There is, however, an essential difference between the two schemes. If certainty is eroded by the presence of non-excluded rivals, and these rivals claim a measurable or rankable standing, the standing of each of these rivals must surely be subject to erosion by the other rivals. By contrast, if standing means freedom in some degree, not from rivals, but from obstruction, this freedom from obstruction can surely be of any degree, even the *perfect* degree, for any number of mutually rival hypotheses without limit?

If we define certainty as a character assigned to the *uniquely possible*, it seems evident that plurality of rival possible things must destroy certainty. Is there something left when certainty has been thus removed from some hypothesis, some suggested answer to some question? Does the presence of rival hypotheses in the individual's thought have an effect expressible as *reducing* an attribute whose extreme degree is certainty? What would be the difference between the individual's attitude to a hypothesis of which he was certain, and one whose certainty was impaired or destroyed by the recognition of other possibilities? If the hypothesis concerned the sequel of a particular course of action, that action might be chosen if the hypothesis were certain, but eschewed if it were not. Can we then say that what is left when certainty has been impaired, is something on whose degree the adoption or eschewal of particular action may depend? When there are plural hypotheses about the outcome of a specified proposed action, will not the rivalry of these hypotheses as counsellors of adoption or eschewal imply their rivalry as claimants to some degree of belief, some degree of imperfect, weakened but positive reliance or confidence? If so, can such belief or reliance be accorded to each of many rival propositions (hypotheses, suggested answers) in a degree, no matter how high, which in no way depends on their plurality, however great? Plainly not. For evidently it cannot be accorded in the *perfect* degree to more than one hypothesis. Must we say that belief, reliance, must in some sense be *shared* amongst rival hypotheses? Must we not say that extra reliance placed upon one hypothesis must be taken away from another, or others? Is not this the implication of our calling the hypotheses rivals? Yet, is there not a strangeness in having positive belief, even in a lessened degree or weakened form and significance, in several ideas which mutually contradict each other, which are in content mutually exclusive? And finally, can we say that something is *shared*, divided out, unless we are able to say what is the total of that shared thing, what is the total of the shares?

This last question has been answered along a line which is, I think it must be said, special to a narrow range of circumstances, and one whose adoption was in a sense fortuitous, yet a line which has become dominant in the context we are concerned with. This line of thought starts from the supposition that rival hypotheses compose a list of 'named' distinct cases, finite in number, and that this list by its meaning is bound to include the hypothesis which will prove true. On this basis, *certainty* can be accorded by the individual to the idea that the truth will be found somewhere in the definite list. The leap of reason is then made: that this certainty, represented by a numeral, unity, is what can be shared out amongst the members of the list. In consequence, the degrees of imperfect belief, the degrees of reliance, are represented by proper fractions which, over the list as a whole, must sum to unity.

What, then, is the ground and justification of that leap? It is a yet more open divorce of the argument from any attachment to strict reason. It declares that because if a mechanical system (tossed coin or dice thrown from a box, et cetera) is subjected many times to some kind of operation, within conditions which allow some variation of circumstance but are themselves in some sense constant, there will be a discernible pattern in the results of these repeated trials, a pattern representable by the proportions of the total number of trials showing this or that class of results. Such a frequency distribution, when many trials in properly bounded conditions have been made and recorded, will be a record of what took place in fact. The distribution will be description, of a particular sort, of the series of operations (trials) as a whole. If a further series of trials is made with an unchanged system within the same bounds of variation of circumstances, it may be argued, with some persuasive force, that the distribution thus obtained will be broadly similar to the former one. The broad character of such distributions, if fresh series continue to be made, will despite indistinctness represent *knowledge* of a sort. What is this knowledge about? What is it knowledge of?

Evidently it is knowledge of a character or propensity belonging to the mechanical system in question, a character which is manifested when that system is repeatedly used in a certain kind of performance. This character is expressible as a distribution of the results of such performances over a number of classes. Can the result of a *single instance* of such performance reflect the character of the distribution which has been recorded for some considerable series of trials? If we find that when a die is repeatedly thrown, each of its six faces appears with roughly equal frequency, can we say that this experience finds expression in any one particular member of the series? It seems evident that it can in no way do so. However, suppose that at each trial two dice are thrown, and after a time the record shows that a total of five dots from the two faces shown in any throw has occurred in about one-ninth of all the throws. Does this justify us in placing more reliance on the suggestion that, in the *next* trial, a total of five will appear, than on the suggestion that, in this same next trial (a 'proper-named' individual trial) a twelve will appear, because in the record a twelve has appeared in only about one thirty-sixth of the instances? If we claim that it does, what practical expression shall we be willing to give, or find justification in giving, to that 'greater reliance'? In answering this question, let us have constantly and sharply before our mind's eye the words 'this particular, proper-named single trial'.

These questions concerning throws of dice illustrate in their own way, and in their own extremely special and restricted context, the dilemma of *epistemic standing*. It is natural, it is plausible to claim that a frequency-distribution of the results of throwing two dice 'tell us something', 'throw light', on the ways the two dice are 'likelier' or less 'likely' to fall in some one identified, particular, proper-named, all-or-nothing throw. But what light? What precise question is answered by the features of a frequency-table, concerning the result of some one intended throw? Does the frequency table answer the question 'How many dots *will show* on the uppermost faces in this proper-named intended throw? Plainly it does not. Does it answer the question: If we made, say, thirty-six thousand throws, how many of them, to a rough approximation, would show a three, or how many a seven? Let us suppose that experiments suggest that it can answer this question. What is the relevance of that answer, when we are concerned with one single identified throw?

The dilemma of epistemic standing is this: If knowledge, relevant and unarguable, is lacking for some question, can that gap be filled by substitutes for knowledge? Can mortal man do the business of life without finding some way of coping with *or else exploiting* a gap of knowledge, an epistemic interval? My answer, which it is one concern of the theme and argument of this book to give, is that he can, and must, *exploit* the creative freedom of his essential, inherent unknowledge of the yet-non-existent content of time-yet-to-come.

Let us turn to the second of our initial questions. Can we speak of the degree to which some hypothesis or suggested answer is obstructed? Are there degrees of possibility?

Possibility, in the sense relevant to our theme, relevant to the business of choice, is a reaction or response of the individual to a suggestion, whether made by himself or another, the suggestion that some specific evolution of affairs as they affect his interest can be the sequel of some course of his own action. If he can discern no obstacle to this evolution, its possibility, in the relevant sense, is perfect. But if an obstacle is visible, the question arises for him whether he can invoke any principle of Nature or any exercise of human ingenuity and resource which might evade or dissolve it. If he can formally imagine such a dissolving of the obstacle, how incongruous does this supposition seem with his accepted lines of thought? Is it hard or easy to assimilate into his Scheme of Things, his conception of the nature and *potentiae* of the field? Such removal of a discerned obstacle may be deemed a shift to the contemplation of a variant of the sequel initially considered, but the variant may attain the same purposes as the other. Possibility is adjudged to a specified course of history-to-come, and such an adjudgement may seem wholly consonant with his scheme of the field, or in various degrees difficult to assimilate to it. In this sense, which is the relevant and effective sense, we may say that there are degrees of possibility. We are not yet asserting that such degrees can be located on any available or creatable metric scale.

Behind the term epistemic standing we can discern two conceptions wholly alien to each other, two attitudes to the experience of men that their choices, in all except trivial matters (and who can say what is trivial?) are made in a darkness fitfully and confusingly lit by the suggestions of the Scheme and the News. One of these attitudes looks on this unknowledge as an adverse circumstance which by taking thought, men can evade or remedy. If we cannot see where we are going (this view holds) we must resort to more powerful illuminants, reason must be applied more subtly to the evidence we possess, in order to extract guidance of what action will conform to what history is going to impose on us. This is the view which sees in some procedure of reckoning or of reason, some form of a probability calculus, a means to overcome the disabilities of men's situation, their need to treat the future as implicit in the past though only confusedly visible in it. The other view is a total discarding of the whole notion that men seek to know a future which awaits them. In this other view, it is the void of time-to-come which must be filled by men's originative thought, by the choices they make amongst the products of imagination, amongst the complex and subtle skeins of choice-dependent seeming possibilities, the Imagined deemed Possible.

In this other view, men *exploit* their unknowledge, the necessary unknowledge of what does not exist, the unknowledge which is the indispensable condition of effective, non-empty, non-powerless, non-illusory choice.

In electing to suppose that choice is in some respect, in some sense, *ex nihilo* origination of history, in electing to deem choice to be effective and not merely responsive, we are evidently committed from the outset of our theme to the second view. Choice *makes a difference*. If so, choice does not merely grope after the pre-existent, it is a *source* of the not-yet-existent. Not all probabilisms, however, are wholly unamenable to such a view, despite their expression in terms which reject it. In his *Treatise on Probability*, J. M. Keynes, encouraged by the words of Leibniz, suggests that a body of evidence which does not suffice for demonstrative proof of a proposition, can none-the-less give it standing as more worthy (so I interpret him) of reliance as a guide to action than rival propositions. Leibniz and Keynes considered that valid rules can be found of *probable inference*, not referring to large classes of instances of mechanical or analogous trials with a system of constant broad character and variable particular state, but relying on reason of a kind:

> In most branches of academic logic – all the arguments aim at demonstrative certainty. They claim to be *conclusive*. But many other arguments are rational and claim some weight, without pretending to be certain. The course which the history of thought has led logic to follow has encouraged the view that doubtful arguments are not within its scope. But in the actual exercise of reason we do not wait on certainty, or deem it irrational to depend on a doubtful argument. If logic investigates the general principles of valid thought, the study of arguments, to which it is rational to attach some weight, is as much a part of it as the study of those which are demonstrative.*

* J. M. Keynes, *A Treatise on Probability* (London: Macmillan 1921) chapter I, page 3.

The ease and grace of Keynes's prose may still our doubts where we ought to put them into words. What is it in an argument that makes it *inconclusive*? Two possible sources of imperfection readily offer themselves. One is the difficulty which may be encountered in transforming impressions (reports from the field) into suitably expressed premisses to serve as a basis of inference. The other is the *absence*, from the body of impressions as a whole, of material which can properly supply some premiss essential to the complete logical construct which would provide a conclusive demonstration. In other words, there may in the first place be doubt as to whether some distinctly formulated proposition, intended to be used as a premiss of argument, properly represents the direct knowledge gained from sense-impressions or experiments. Keynes, as he makes clear in section 2 of his first chapter, is not concerned with this first possible source of trouble. He assumes that there is in the mind of the person who is adjudging probability a body of propositions which he takes to be *knowledge*. It is the insufficiency of this body of knowledge, as a means of establishing some conclusion, that concerns him. If the adjudger of probability had some one or more additional premiss, his argument would be conclusive. So, at least, I read the meaning of the first page of Keynes's chapter 1. Now we have to ask: If there is need of some additional premiss, how can the existing premisses, which are *independent* of the missing one, supply the means of filling the gap? Plainly, I would say, they cannot. The gap must be filled by an exercise of the individual's originative audacity. He must invent, or at least assume with a degree of arbitrary initiative, a premiss which, if available to him, would complete the basis of a *demonstrative* argument. Thus we are, after all, in the terrain of imaginative creation, the terrain of figment. Probable inference is inference based on improvised, suppositious premisses, which when added to those derivable from what is taken to be knowledge from the field, compose a demonstrative argument.

Men make choices of action. Keynes's tacit assumption is that these are grounded with care and skill in the body of seemingly relevant knowledge that the chooser possesses; that this body of knowledge, whatever its 'amount' (should we say, degree of adequacy or insufficiency?) if properly consulted, will give guidance about the links between actions and their sequels, such that choice can be 'rational', and he seems to appeal to the fact that choices of action are commonly based on knowledge insufficient to demonstrate with certainty what will be the outcome of a given action, as proof that a logic of probable inference exists and is known to and applied by men in the ordinary business of life. Can this claim be accepted?

Do not men rather, when obliged to choose in face of unknowledge, allow the News to suggest to them the whole of an evolution of affairs of which it has provided mere glimpses of the opening scenes? Men act, not upon calculation but upon suggestion, building upon foundations which they conjure from one of many or infinitely many possible interpretations of what they see. What evidence does the history of men's efforts show, to support the supposition that rational inference, that is, *successful* inference, is consistently possible in the tempest of the world's affairs? Men of genius have sometimes built history in the image of their own ambitions, for a time, by inspiring others to see some reflection of their own thoughts. But is this a proof of the validity of *rational probable belief*? Even the vast achievement of natural science shows, perhaps, the effect of audacious pursuit of suggestion by imagination, rather than the 'correctly' calculated steps of a journey to a goal.

Keynes's approach to the question of *knowledge insufficient for certainty* (that is, for uniqueness of the answer entertained to some question) is to me far more appealing than that which starts from the notion of relative frequency. Keynes does not require some degree or other of positive, though 'imperfect', reliance to be placed on each of several mutually rival propositions. It is true that when the mutually exclusive propositions which can, within the constraints of some formal system, be entertained as answers to a question concerning this system, compose a finite list which is, by the nature of the system, seen to be complete, Keynes would require the numerical measures of the respective degrees of reliance (if such could be determined) to sum to unity, unity then representing the certainty that the true answer was a member of the list. This requirement is perhaps deemed, in his theory as in other versions of probability, to be a necessary condition of consistency, of coherence. But does not the notion itself of degrees of positive reliance placed on mutually exclusive answers to some question already infringe reason? To ask this leads us to ask what is the meaning, what is the basis and validity of the implied guidance, to be found in a statement that one proposition out of several rival, mutually exclusive ones all offering their respective answers to the same question, has a greater probability than another, let alone that it has a probability of one quarter, or one tenth? What are we essentially told by such a statement? Or we can ask what answer, subsequently given as a report from the field, would *refute* any one such probability statement? If an action-chooser claims to rely, to the extent of one-quarter, on some specific sequel to his action, can we say, when this sequel fails to be realized, that the assigned probability was false? Or again, can a man who had assigned a high probability, but not certainty, to some specific sequel, console himself, in case of its failure, by the thought that in some sense his assignment of probability was 'justified by the rules', or was 'rational'?

The requirement that the probabilities assigned to an exhaustive list of contingent results of some 'experiment' should sum to unity derives from the relative-frequency notion of probability, and that notion has no legitimate reference to single, identified, 'proper-named' instances of a trial performance such as must result in one or other of the contingent results; for *frequency* refers to a *numerous class* of such trials, where one particular trial may prove to yield one contingent result and another particular trial may yield a different contingency, so that every contingency in the list will, if there are 'enough' trials, be represented in some particular proportion of cases. How are the proportions to be discovered? There must, in one or other of two senses, be a *counting of cases*. Either a numerous class of trials must actually be made and their results recorded, or the pattern which would result from such a class must be inferred from an inspection of the structure of the mechanical or other system in question. Either way requires an experience, or a notional possibility of numerous trials. How can it have meaning or application when only one single trial is made or contemplated?

Keynes subscribes to the view that coherence of thought requires the probabilities assigned to (as I prefer to say) rival answers to one question, or in a narrower context, rival outcomes of one proper-named trial of, say, a physical system, if by some procedure they can be expressed as numbers, to sum to unity. I have suggested already that coherence is in any case questionable when *mutually exclusive* answers are each assigned some degree of positive reliance. Can one, in any intelligible sense, half-believe in one thing and half-believe in its contradictory? The form of words, even if not at odds with itself, seems empty. But if it were not, do we not severely handicap ourselves by adopting, for the expression of epistemic standing, a means which makes the standing assignable to one member of a list of hypotheses depend on the *number* of rival hypotheses?

Discussion of the theme of epistemic standing is confused by its ambiguous purposes. Are we seeking a way to put out of sight the fact of unknowledge of the sequels of rival courses of action that seem within reach? If so, probability is a word serving only as an incantation. Having uttered it, we then turn our backs on the whole matter, and proceed in our study of choice (of action or policy) as if the rival choosables were offered by some agency independent of the thinking being; were offered as things each completely specified in all respects relevant to the interests of the chooser, and had merely to be glanced at by him, in order to elicit from him, in view of his tastes and endowments, an automatic election of one of them. Or are we willing to suppose that all activities of men are equivalent in nature to the endless throwing of dice, where the relevant question is not 'What will be the outcome of the throw which will be made at, say, 8 a.m. on 16 December 1976, but 'What will be the frequency-table of results obtained by the throwing of the dice steadily in an unchanging frame of general conditions from now until a month hence? These fore-going attitudes are not an effort to penetrate the question of choice in face of unknowledge, but a resolve to ignore it. In absolute contrast, we can see men as engaged in filling a void, the void of time-to-come, by an exertion of originative power of an extreme kind, the imaginative genesis of history. If so, we shall not think of the epistemic gap as a mountain to be climbed until at the summit we are above the mists, but as an alluvial plain whose boundaries in the horizontal dimension we seek to define in order to know what freedom the stream of history has, to flow in this or that meander.

My proposal is to turn upside-down the orthodox effort to find for each rival hypothesis in a finite list of such, a degree of positive claim to be the destined truth, and instead of this, to suppose the action-chooser to be engaged in imagining the course of things, which might follow a specified action of his own, in a series of variant forms limited in number only by his own need to meet a deadline of decision. He is a dramaturge, a playwright of history, able not only to choose one action course from among many that seem within his reach, but to originate for each such action a skein of imagined sequels, unconfined in number by any nature of their own, and subject only to one condition, their being *possible*. The relevant meaning of epistemic standing, for the business of choice, is freedom from discerned disabilities, freedom from visible obstruction. Who can know what *will* be? Nobody. Let us then use the freedom of unknowledge to imagine what can be, of good and bad, as the sequel to each choosable plan of action. Choice is amongst skeins of possibilities, the Imagined, deemed Possible.

)))
The uncompletable skein
and its implications
(((

W HEN WE OPT for the supposition that choice brings into being, and into effect, something that was not implicit in the antecedents, we are transforming the essence and foundation of the question we have sought to epitomize by the phrase 'the epistemic interval'. For by supposing choice to be a *beginning*, a cut in the texture of history, the sudden presence, amongst the impulses from which history is formed, of something which did not exist until the chooser's present moment of choosing, we deny ourselves the resort to the notion that the sequels of any choice are a finite set of entities given in character and in number from outside the chooser's thought. There is an absolute contrast, on whose fundamental importance we are bound to insist, between the notion of an externally given, 'ready-made', set of possible sequels of an action, on the one hand, and on the other, the notion of an inexhaustible originative source of imagined sequels, unconfined in number by the antecedents of the chooser's present. The notion of an epistemic interval whose contents could be listed and relevantly described, not only by the chooser in reference to the state of his imaginative process in his present, but by the detached analyst as a matter independent of the date when this listing was done, and depending only on some description of a mechanical or quasi-mechanical system, no doubt stems from the games of chance which led to the formulation of a theory of probability. In general, apart from the context of a game with stated rules which imply that all the respective outcomes of instances of the game can be classified under certain headings, such as 'heads' or 'tails', what

ground have we for placing any limit on the variety of the contents of the epistemic interval, the 'interval of unknowledge'?
Originative choice must surely be deemed a *business* or a *process*,
something which, even when arrested by a deadline, is conscious
of the incompleteness of the process and its essential *uncompletability in principle and nature*.

Probability names a collection of attitudes of mind, of conceptions, ascendant ideas, principles, theories and systems which
can find hardly any thread uniting them all, except the action-
chooser's insistent consciousness of the epistemic interval, his
experience of states of mind which are not perfect knowledge nor
yet entire freedom from suggestion and thrusting influences upon
his course of thought. To attain for some question a conclusion or
answer, concerning which a man can say 'This only can be the
truth of this matter' is perhaps rare. To feel that a question, even
if its terms are understood, presents a total blank and elicits from
his scheme of the world no suggestion or glimpse of a path to
follow, is surely rarer still. We are mostly confronted by plurality,
rivalry and contradiction. 'Probability' names most of the attempts
which have been made to fill this anarchic region, but it also names
ideas which have no business in that region. The attempt to fill
the region of unknowledge or of fragmentary knowledge, with
ideas which are part of the structure of knowledge itself, the
assumption that essential unknowledge can be conjured out of
existence by an arithmetical formula, arose perhaps from the
inveteracy of the card-turners' or dice-throwers' obsession. Such
players do not make one throw and then abandon the dice for
ever. They are not concerned with what we have called a non-
divisible non-seriable experiment. They have before them, consciously or unconsciously, an intention to continue play, to continue making trials with an unchanging apparatus according to
unchanging rules, indefinitely. Only if the game and its fluctuations
pall, and the player revives its interest by a sudden increase in the
stakes, can a throw take on a once-for-all character. But if he
makes a throw with an uniquely large stake, that throw becomes

thereby unique. If a throw is unique, can a frequency-table apply to it, or serve as a guide to its outcome?

If, in any present, the frequency-tables resulting from a 'long' course of play have shown some stability, those frequencies can, perhaps, count as knowledge in relation to an intended long course of play to be pursued in time-to-come. They will be useful knowledge for the players, as long as these players intend to adhere to roughly uniform stakes. For thus the intended course of play will become a divisible experiment. For the inveterate players, however, there is an evident danger that *the distinction may be lost* between the unique once-for-all, proper-named and never-to-be repeated trial, where there can be no meaningful application of relative frequency because there is no plurality, on one hand; and on the other, the intention and practicability of indefinite repetition under relevantly unchanging rules and confinements of variation, where relative frequencies recorded in the past may have a claim to be knowledge for a divisible experiment in time-to-come. For the student of the nature of choice, however, the distinction must not be lost, for it is vital and essential.

Probability, as a set of conceptions arising from games of chance, formal games where what can relevantly happen is laid down as a definite, specific and finite list of classes of contingencies, such that any contingency, any result of play, can be easily and simply classified: probability in this sense has been a distracting and misleading influence on the study of that aspect of the human condition which we have sought to label 'the epistemic interval'. This unsuitability, or irrelevance, of the probability notions derived from games of chance, to the unknowledge which affects choice, has two main constituents. One of these is the very questionable propriety, or meaningfulness, of seeking guidance about the outcome of a *single* (let us say, unique) *proper-named and identified* trial of a mechanical or quasi-mechanical system, such as cutting packs of cards or throwing dice, from a frequency-table whose derivation and nature rest wholly on a *plurality* of trials. The other respect in which games of chance fulfil a condition which effective, originative choice cannot fulfil concerns the number of distinct items to which probabilities need be assigned. In games of chance this number is finite and specific. It is dictated by the rules of the game, such as the rule which requires the dice-thrower to count the total of dots on the uppermost faces of the two dice which he has thrown. Such rules ensure the practicable *complete listing* of all relevantly distinct outcomes which can result from any one 'play'. In the business of originative choice, how can we conceive that every possible discrete product of imagination could be finitely listed? Yet if the chooser is conscious of his own endless capacity to add to the variety of his imagined sequels of some one choosable course of action, what meaning can he assign to a *distribution*, over the items of a list recognized to be incomplete and uncompletable, of a quantity representing the *certainty* that the eventual truth will be one of the sequels he has, at some present, *already* conceived and listed?

Does a proposition derive epistemic standing from its membership of a group of propositions amongst which the truth must logically be found, or does that standing arise from a consideration of its own character against the background of a general body of knowledge? Keynes's degree of rational belief belonged to this second conception. It represented the relation of the particular proposition, to a body of other propositions, not competing with this one to answer a given question, but expressing matters, principles or circumstances bearing on the claim of this proposition to be the truth. Keynes claimed that between such a body of 'evidence' or 'direct knowledge' and the proposition to which it was deemed relevant, there would subsist some relation that could, in a new but valid sense, be called logical. The degree of rational belief in the proposition could, of course, be different if the body of evidence was different. But there seems to be no suggestion that it would be altered by the formulation of other propositions claiming to answer the same question. Keynes does not, I think, consider, or refer to, a proposition as the *answer to a question*. This view, which seems to me always suggestively illuminating, carries my argument outside Keynes's concern. By contrast with the independence from competing propositions, which a proposition claiming a degree of rational belief, in Keynes's manner, can perhaps assert, the claim based on relative frequency is subject to the number of competing propositions, where any change in which number can affect the probability accorded to the proposition. In this light, the foundation on which any claim to probability through frequency must rest seems mechanical and distinctly alien to the notion which I seek to label *epistemic* standing. It is perhaps questionable whether a degree of rational belief can be quite unaffected by the formulation of additional competing propositions, since such formulation might be excluded unless there were a change in the body of relevant evidence.

The standing (if I may use my own term) which Keynes's approach would confer on a proposition is still of the kind that I would call *positive* reliance or confidence. It is *belief*, though imperfect. By contrast, I am proposing absence of disbelief as the highest degree of standing, and various degrees of declension from this complete absence of epistemic obstruction, as other degrees of standing. When the list of propositions (for us, the list of imagined sequels of a choice of action) seems able in principle to be endlessly augmented, zero disbelief, and other less complete exemptions from disbelief, offer an index of standing which is independent of the number of rival propositions which have been or may be thought of. My claim for such a meaning for epistemic standing rests on its natural assimilation in a world of effective choice, since this is a world of *essential unknowledge*.

)))
Disbelief: the measure of
possibility inverted
(((

C H O I C E I S A business of the whole psyche. It involves intellection
of sense-impressions and their assimilation to a scheme or geometry (coherent account) of a supposed field outside the thinking
being's thought; the origination of imagined paths of history out
of the abstract permanent elements which compose the scheme of
the field, paths unrealized and unreported, but deemed possible in
their freedom from discerned obstruction; the location of these
paths as rival suggestions of the content of time-to-come, the time
which is the inferred, invented consequence of the transience of
thought, the transience of the present, the time which is a space
accommodating succession. It involves the sorting of such paths
into skeins each presupposing some initiating course of action on
the part of the chooser; the comparison of such skeins in respect
of the imaginative delight and distress to which each, by its best
and worst comprised possibilities, exposes the chooser's instinct
of *experience by imagination*; and his self-commitment to that course
which offers in highest degree a good state of mind. To propose a
formal representation of this complex, subtle, involved and elusive
activity is a temerity only excused by the need, which the natural
bent and gifts of mankind and their historical experience have
thrust upon them, for a formal instrument by which to grasp the
nature and meaning of things. The claims of such a construct are
not those of truth discovered, but of something made; an obedience, in a humble mode, to something like the instinct which
drives the poet.

To be the means of delight by imagination, or of that distress by imagination, some degree of which will be the price of delight, a path of history envisaged as the sequel of some action within the chooser's reach is required to seem to him *possible*, that is, not fatally obstructed within his knowledge. If such a sequel is entirely unobstructed, wholly free, within the chooser's thought, of any threatened interference, we can say that it is for him *perfectly possible*.

In an earlier chapter we considered the expression *epistemic interval*. We implied two possible definitions. The first of these would take *certainty* concerning some proposition, acceptance of it as the *uniquely* valid answer to some question, as one boundary of such an interval, and *exclusion*, denial of the validity of the proposition, as the other boundary. If we then assume that the interval is something which can be divided and subdivided into a scale, and that it can thus provide the range of a variable, that variable should presumably represent by its increasing numerical values an approach towards certainty. Let us, however, free ourselves from the whole of this frame of thought, re-define the nature of the interval and turn upside-down the variable for which we deem it to provide a range. Instead of *certainty*, that is, *unique* acceptability of the proposition whose epistemic standing we are concerned with, let us take as one boundary of the epistemic interval the *perfect possibility* of the proposition. By contrast with certainty, perfect possibility need not be confined to a sole and unique answer to some question. If we take choice to be a beginning in our sense, no one answer can be the sole perfectly possible answer to the question: What will be the sequel if I do this, or this? Possibility is an adjudgement of the chooser according to his knowledge, and his recognition of choices-to-come renders that knowledge quite incapable of excluding all but one sequel to a specific action. Perfect possibility can in abstract principle be accorded to each proposition in an endlessly extensible list. Only a deadline for decision need cut off the process of extending it. Then, what character for the *epistemic variable* will give it the utmost efficiency for its purpose?

86

If the extreme degree of possibility is to be assigned to each item of an ever-extensible list, its formal representation ought to allow of this continuing extension without the need for continual adjustment of the values of the epistemic variable already assigned to items of the list. The value assigned to any item ought, that is to say, to be independent of the number of other items which, at any stage, compose the list. In particular, this means for example that the values of the epistemic variable assigned to the answers pro-posed for some one question ought not to be required, by their formal nature and meaning, to sum to any particular total. If perfect possibility itself is assignable to an unlimited number of answers at once, so ought to be that unchanging value of the representative variable which stands for perfect possibility. If we represent increasing possibility by decreasing values of the variable, so that *perfect possibility* is represented by its *zero* value, our con-dition will be met.

Our formal scheme, designed to admit to our thought degrees of epistemic standing other than the two absolutes of perfect possibility and entire exclusion, now comprises the notions of an epistemic interval bounded by those absolutes, an epistemic variable whose range is that interval, and the prescription that this variable shall decrease towards increasingly unobstructed possi-bility of the proposition being considered, so that perfect possi-bility is represented by its zero value. An arbitrary value of the variable will stand for perfect adjudged *impossibility*. This scheme is so far purely formal. Can we find any interpretation of it which will link it naturally to the intuitions or the feelings of our thinking being? Can it be made to touch the keys on our keyboard of experience?

Pure intellections if there are such, thoughts completely describ-able in terms of form, do not very readily lend themselves to measurement. They do not in their essential nature seem to have either extension or intensity. What is measurable in some sense in connection with thoughts is feeling of some sort. Feeling quite evidently has a range of intensities. Then can *possibility* be linked to *feeling* of some sort? The feeling in whose engenderment possibility-judgements can play a part is that of *surprise*. A report from the field, which had been judged impossible, causes an extreme degree of surprise. No feeling of surprise will be engendered by a report which was deemed perfectly possible. We must be on guard here in one respect. Surprise can be the sequel of either of two kinds of report. A report, an event or transformation, which had been imagined and rejected as not possible, which is received in fact, will cause surprise. But so also will one which had not ever entered into the individual's imagination, which had never been conceived or considered. Novelty, the *unexpected*, can cause surprise as well as the *counter-expected*. In seeking an emotional reflection of judgements of possibility, we are concerned with the counter-expected. What is novel may be counter-expected, but it may instead be simply unthought of.

The suggestion of potential surprise as a means of providing possibility with a scale requires more than the identifying of a judgement of perfect possibility with the notion of *nil* exposure to surprise in case the proposition or imagined report proves valid. We have to find a means of dividing and sub-dividing the epistemic interval, in its guise of an interval between a zero intensity and an absolute maximum intensity of potential surprise, into a scale with a definite operational meaning.

The practicability of such a scale will be a matter of the use for which it is required. If our chooser is credited with analytical habits of thought, such a scale will be for him a needed tool, but it will by no means need to be either publicly observable and recognizable by other persons, or to have, even for the chooser, any high degree of stability from one present moment to another. Let us here insist again on the *solitary* status and nature of the present moment. Each present fills the chooser's universe. There is nothing else, for him, but his present thought, his present moment. No two present moments can for him co-exist, the idea of such a plurality is self-contradictory. Thus the scale of feeling, representing judgements of possibility, is for *now*. In regard to it,

88

moments-to-come must take care of themselves. The chooser will rest his construction of such a scale on remembered experiences which he may reasonably assume to have a lasting meaning for him, and he may accordingly ascribe some permanence to the scale itself. But even if he does not assign any meaning to such permanence or stability, what can he do? We are prisoners of the present who must choose in the present on the basis of our present knowledge, judgements and assessments.

We have spoken of dividing up the epistemic interval by a scale, that is, by a series of sub-intervals equal to each other in some operational sense. It may be that this is an unnecessarily and unnaturally refined notion. A man knows where he is in a familiar countryside by noting landmarks which need by no means be equally spaced from each other. Intensities of potential surprise will perhaps present themselves to the chooser as instances of actual remembered experience, though the assessment may be somewhat complicated by the relatively greater or less importance of the matter at issue. A highly astonishing report from the field, in a seemingly trivial matter, may make no deeper impression on memory than a more ordinary surprise concerning something recognizably vital. However, the source of a strong remembered impression will surely be resolvable into the two components, answering respectively the questions: How surprising? and: How important? The presence, in the chooser's epistemic interval, considered as the range of a variable potential surprise, of landmarks of some sort, whether resting on individual remembered instances or left in memory as the residuum of a life's experience, may be all that is needed to make potential surprise a practical means of thought. Such considerations seem more apt to Nature and experience than such proposals as dividing the initial interval into halves by finding a point which is psychically equi-distant from the two extremities of the interval, then subdividing each half in a similar manner, and so on.

If the chooser, by means of such landmarks, can assess the intensity of surprise which a specific report from the field would occasion him as very high, very slight, rather unusual, and so on, this may serve his practical need, which is to modify the influence on his business of choice exerted by some imagined sequel considered purely in its desiredness or counter-desiredness and not at all in its possibility. In this way, the effective 'edges of the possible', the boundaries of a skein of imagined sequels of some available course of action, may be defined so as to recognize an inter-action, in the chooser's business of choice, between degrees of desiredness and degrees of possibility. An imagined sequel, if desirable enough, may exert some influence on choice despite its not being wholly free of discernible obstruction, despite its not being judged *perfectly* possible. Do we really exclude from consideration all but the *perfect* possibilities? That we do not, seems even more evident with counter-desired than with positively desired sequels. For a sequel which would be a disaster, crippling action and hopes for times beyond, will be menacing and alarming in some degree unless it can be excluded entirely. The epistemic interval will not be a forbidden territory or no-man's-land, the thoughts that stray into it will surely be given some audience during the business of choice, and thus the means of assessing and expressing degrees of possibility less than perfect are a needed practical tool.

Like time with which it is so intimately and uniquely involved, knowledge is *sui generis* in a peculiarly extreme and fundamental sense. It can be received by consciousness but not deliberately ejected from consciousness. Its fresh items, the News, are each liable to transform the import and bearing of all previously gained knowledge, which is in the last degree vulnerable and mutable in its details concerned with circumstance. The conformation of knowledge is its essence, it is a design and not a homogeneous stuff whose 'quantity' can be meaningfully defined. Is it strange that knowledge cannot be treated like the contents of a grocer's shop? Such thoughts must cause us misgivings about the whole policy of seeking to make epistemic standing a variable rather than an absolute 'possible' or 'excluded'. The most austere method of showing epistemic standing in operation in the business of choice of action is to assign it this meaning of an absolute, and consider what are the consequences when all hypothetical sequels of any action are regarded simply as either 'possible' or 'impossible'. Yet this method would dismiss from consideration a whole area of consciousness. All that we refer to by such terms as doubt, indecision, precarious hope, would be excluded from our formal representation of the business of choice. Moreover those states of mind are part of the fibre of the business of choice. How could choice be described as a 'business' if we supposed that sequels of a contemplated course of action were no sooner conceived than assigned to the absolute categories of 'possible' or 'impossible'? This forming of judgements of possibility will be arduous and must be accomplished step-by-step. In our theme *possibility* means the absence of obstacles, in the chooser's knowledge and thought, to the complete imagining of all circumstances and transformations of circumstance, all such actions-to-come by others, the timely provision of all indispensable resources, as are required and involved in the evolution of affairs which he is assessing. This complete imagining may itself be impracticable within any acceptable deadline of decision. But the chooser, if he is to attain that good state of mind which is the real and seizable aim of the business of decision, must satisfy his practical conscience that he has examined the question of possibility so far and fully as he can. He must search for obstacles that need by no means be obvious. He must in thought traverse the route of the imagined course of affairs and see that it is clear. While such search and examination are in process, however instantly ready for each turn and contingency of this inspection the prepared mind may be, the chooser's state of thought will be that of unfinished business, of doubt, unreadiness to give judgement. Such a state of thought will not, in the midst of the tide of affairs, be a merely occasional or exceptional one, but the stuff of the human condition. To confine our theory to the absolutes, to the *completed state* of the chooser's examination of possibility, would be to take that road with which economics has largely been content, to assume that the 'chooser' (if orthodox economic analysis can call him such) is in some way bound to arrive at conclusions correctly based upon relevantly complete knowledge, and to absolve itself from any effort to explain how such knowledge is secured. We have to explain how the chooser seeks his desires, not how he recognizes some 'objective' goal when it has been inexplicably attained.

The epistemic interval, some formal frame and apparatus by which the business of choice can be seen as the chooser's mode of *exploiting the freedom of unknowledge* (the essential unknowledge of what waits to be originated, partly by this exploitation), of making possibility, absence of epistemic obstruction, the test and satisfying principle of practical conscience, is central and essential to our theme. The epistemic interval is not a means of making concessions or slight accommodations by which a model of human conduct, which ascribes that conduct to fully-informed reason, can be brought into some contact with human fallibility and the imperfections of experienced, as distinct from ideal, rationality. It is a rejection and dismissal of that model, in a sense too fundamental to be easily made plain. The epistemic interval, the void of unknowledge, the solitariness of the present, the sole reality of the new, the transient, the original: these expressions are meant as the vessel of a conception of choice which overturns the primacy or the exclusive validity of problem-solving choice, and declares that the question which choice must answer is not: Which of these given, listed things shall we do? but: What shall exist? What history shall be made in the void? Let me add one remark to these intransigent heresies. They are not claims to an understanding of the transcendent. My theme is concerned only with how things appear to men. It is not an irreverence.

)))
*A formal representation of
the business of choice*
(((

In its manifold complexity, the theme of choice offers us two policies: to see what follows logically from some formal statement of the matter, and to use all the richness of intuition in a picture where almost every face of human nature, the human predicament, the endless suggestions of history and our institutional frame will have some place. The two methods are indispensable to each other. Any formal statement of what is involved in the business of choice must be founded on a consideration of the human predicament, the answers to the questions: What do we directly and immediately know, what can we do, what difference can we make, and what is the locus of any such doing? These questions are to be taken at their most fundamental, freed so far as we can manage it from any casual or superficial assumptions or conditioning of thought. The essential nature of the human affair is what we seek when we ask: What is time? In a sense, our four questions come together in this one.

What we directly, immediately (without the mediation of anything) know is thought. If there is not thought, there is nothing. The universal inference is a thinking being. Each of us casts himself in this role, and is for his own purposes *the* thinking being. What are his thoughts about? We (each for himself) postulate a source of impressions, the field. Concerning it we devise a scheme or geometry. *Res cogitans* thinks about *res extensa*. But what is thought like? Can such a question be answered? Thought is unique, how can it be likened to anything else? However, thought conveys an irresistible intuition. It is transient. A thought takes place, and yields place, and this arrival and departure are a unity. Time is the transience of thought. If these statements can be said to fit together, that is no doubt all we can claim for them.

The formal frame which these ideas supply is, at the sparest minimum, that of a present moment of thought, encompassing all that *is*, taking place by the very fact of being transformed into a different present. Is this transience illusion or reality? Is time the truth, or is it a delusion suffered by human consciousness as it scans 'inch by inch' a picture where all history co-exists in eternity? In such a picture, choice would be as passive, infertile and inert as any other detail, merely something that exists. But this is not how choice appears to us in the business of life. The choice which is interesting to study is at the opposite pole from the notion of a vacuous link between distinct locations in the picture of an event-less history determinate to the last detail. Choice is interesting if we elect to deem it to be (short of things transcending knowledge) the *ne plus ultra* of explanation of history. Choice is interesting if we acknowledge it to bring thought to a stop, so that we suppose in it an element which cannot be referred or whose genesis cannot be ascribed to antecedents. Originative choice is what I have ventured to label a *beginning*. From this there follows a paradox.

A beginning, in this special sense, being exempt from ante-cedents which would account for it entire, is unforeknowable con-cerning its character (its form) and the calendar date when it may occur. A beginning in this special sense is something partly un-caused. But the word *beginning* is meant to suggest more than this. Beginning is the beginning of something, it has ascribed to it a sequel, it has an effect, it makes a difference. What difference will a particular choice make? There is evidently no such thing as a particular choice until that choice has taken place, what difference it will make is as unforeknowable as the character of the choice itself. What will it *make a difference to*? The sequels of all previous choices. Those sequels, then, are themselves in some degree unfore-knowable. But what, then, is the use of choice, if its sequel cannot be known? Does choice, in this case, mean what the word means in ordinary, unselfconscious discourse? Can choice whose outcome is not foreknown be properly called choice at all?

In these passages I have sought to outline what appears to me as the paradox of choice, the paradox of an act of thought and of commitment whose incentive is to *make a difference*, in small or momentous matters, to subsequent history, yet which must be made in unknowledge of what that difference will prove to be. This unknowledge is not absolute. The chooser, we suppose, has his scheme or geometry of natural principles which set the bounds of *natural possibility*. He has some picture of the particular contingent state to which history has brought 'the present', a set of circumstances which, within the bounds of natural possibility, impose the limits of *general possibility*, the totality of all the skeins of imaginable sequels of the choices of action open to him, for which sequels he can discern no fatal obstacles. What he can choose from this array of general possibility is a skein of *special possibilities*, the mutually rival imagined sequels which some one choice of action seems to leave not discernibly obstructed but which other choices would exclude. If so, what extension of our minimum formal description of the human predicament will best help us to be orderly in thought about *paradoxical originative choice*, choice amongst choosables which are works of the chooser's own imagination, though employing means suggested by the News from the field?

We need first to set out succinctly the array of peculiar difficulties with which the attempt to understand such a business of choice confronts us. But there is an encouragement for this attempt. The chooser himself is obliged to reduce his business to an orderly procedure, whether consciously or not, if he is to perform it. The difficulties can be seen in two steps of thought. At first, let us be content with the supposition that the chooser distributes his imagined sequels of any choice under the two absolute headings of 'possible' and 'excluded'. Then in comparing the respective skeins of sequels of two rival courses of action, he may find that to choose course A gives him imaginative access to a more brilliant hope than any offered by course B, but also exposes him to a worse threat than any arising from B. Moreover, we must ask what influence is exerted upon him by the 'interior' members of each skein, those sequels which are neither the 'best' nor the 'worst' in the skein. If we can show by what steps of thought the chooser can bring his tastes to bear on a sufficiently epitomized account of each of the rival skeins, we shall have dealt with one fundamental difficulty. But then, we are obliged to consider what will flow from our admitting the reality and practical bearing of an *epistemic interval* with some content of sequels which are judged neither perfectly possible nor quite excluded. We have, in fact, to show how the chooser can cope with unknowledge under two guises, or in two forms. Unknowledge can confront him in the form of mere plurality of equi-possible sequels, all other sequels being dismissed as impossible. Or unknowledge can present itself in the form of a judgement that a particular sequel is obstructed in its power of being realized, but in a way which offers some hint that the obstacle may be removed. Unknowledge can thus confront the chooser in the form of imperfect or doubtful possibility. We shall seek to show that these two forms or faces of unknowledge can be given one and the same type of expression.

In seeking as we have just done to provide a main frame of ideas concerning the chooser's task, we have left aside a question which was touched on in earlier chapters, the question how the chooser reduces to some basis of comparability the complex sequels or paths of evolution of affairs which he imagines and deems possible. The ultimate process of assessment of a sequel in terms of desiredness or counter-desiredness, or in a different terminology, the process of valuation, is beyond the reach of analysis by any apparatus which the formal theoretician as such disposes of. The chooser has tastes, criteria or tests which he applies intuitively. They may not be applied to a sequel directly in its full complexity. It is conceivable that some situation, some state of affairs imagined to be attained at some calendar-point, may serve as a symbol or summary of the quality of the sequel as a whole. Or in some other way, a symbol may be substituted by the chooser for the sequel in all its detail, and this symbol may be the thing to which valuation is applied.

It is not without good reason that humanity has adopted the metrical conception and convention, the convention that we can very generally ask with practical meaning, and answer with good effect, the question, How much? To adopt this convention, in regard to any subject-matter, is to claim that we can say, of two instances of this subject-matter, that one of them is, as it were, further along the road than the other; and that we can go beyond that statement, and say of three instances of this subject-matter, that c is further along the road than b, and that b is further along the road than a, and that the distance of c from b is, let us say, 'more important' than that of b from a. For this latter statement can be glossed as follows. We will think of a second 'road', on which *points* shall represent the *distances* we discerned on the first road. Then we can say, for example, that the distance on the first road from b to c is represented by a point further along the second road than the point on that road which represents the distance on the first road, from a to b. When we can compare, not only relative *positions* on the first road, but relative *differences* of position on that road, we are in some sense performing measurement. For when we can compare differences, and say that one is 'more important' than another, we can seek two differences which are *equal* in 'importance'. We can thus divide any interval of the subject-matter into halves, we can halve each of these halves, and so on. We can sub-divide the interval into a scale of equal sub-intervals. It may sometimes be the case that this sub-division can in principle be carried to any degree of fineness, without limit, as lengths marked on a straight line from some arbitrary point can represent the real-number continuum. In practice it seems difficult to conceive of sub-division being carried further and further without limit; but in practice also, it may very often be plain that beyond some degree of fineness, further refinement would be useless and inapplicable.

In these chapters we have reached the conclusion, though by a highly unorthodox route, that choice involves valuation. If the choosables were each of them impenetrable to the chooser, so that he could simply say that he liked one of them more, or disliked it less, than another, without feeling the need or possibility of any insight into the basis of these preferences, this supposition would absolve the chooser, and the analyst, from any need of a scale of desiredness or counter-desiredness. But on the contrary, my theme seeks to suggest an internal structure for each choosable, which involves the business of choice in an intellective process. Each skein of imagined sequels must be conceived and constructed by the chooser, the individual sequels must be formed in imagination and examined as to their possibility, and then as to their desiredness or its opposite. The comparison of rival skeins (the rival choosables) thus seems to require valuation of individual sequels. The approach we have adopted above to the question of the meaning and construction of a scale seeks to be psychically direct and general enough to allow us to use the language of valuation and of measurement in a formal representation of the business of choice.

Let us then return to the two steps of thought that we distinguished above. In the first, we supposed the chooser to assign all the sequels he imagines for some course of action to an absolute 'possible' or an absolute 'excluded' category. Those he excludes as fatally obstructed can have no influence on his choice. The rest are for him, by our supposition, equi-possible. We are supposing him able to place each of these sequels on a scale of desiredness: counter-desiredness. We have now to ask, what is the nature and bearing of the distinction between desiredness and counter-desiredness. Ought we simply to speak of greater or less desiredness? Can there be, or must there be, in the midst of any skein of sequels assessed for their degrees of desiredness, some place, perhaps some particular sequel, which divides the positively desired from the positively counter-desired sequels? It seems there must be such a point, related to our conception of choice as the pursuit of imagination by action, the notion of choice as *enterprise*. For amongst the rival courses of action that present themselves to the chooser's thought, there will be some which suggest a wide diversity of possible sequels from very much desired to very strongly disliked, or in more colourless terms, sequels stretching over a large range of the scale of desiredness; and there will be some whose range of diversity of sequels is small. What will this difference of diversity or of range of desiredness depend on? Will it not be a function of the degree of novelty, of advance across untrodden ground, which informs the course of action? Will not the diversity of the sequels imagined and deemed possible be greater, on the whole, the greater the intellectual daring and 'high nerve' embodied in the action-course, the *enterprise*? To be enterprising is to embrace the unknowledge which consists in plurality and diversity of envisaged possible outcomes. Thus we can suggest that a very narrow range of such diversity, attained by the choice of an action-course which does not far overstep the limits of experience and familiarity, can be regarded as the *neutral* level of desiredness. In the extreme, it is the one which will broadly correspond to 'doing nothing', to allowing the inertial instincts of life to hold sway. We may say that the neutral sequel or narrow range of sequels is the one which is *easily* brought within imaginative, anticipative reach. Again in familiar language, we can suppose the chooser to have available a 'safe' course of action, one which will seem to expose him to small success and small misfortune; to depart from this available course, to choose one which suggests a brilliant and also a disastrous sequel, will be to force upon himself a comparison, namely, that of the safety he could have had with the disaster which 'high enterprise' will thrust upon his imagination. Is it not this comparison which renders positively counter-desirable the disaster which, by a 'safe' choice, he could have excluded?

When all the sequels, which the chooser has envisaged for some course of action, are treated by him as either equi-possible with one another or as fatally obstructed and impossible, which are the ones that will most strongly arrest his attention? They will belong, by compulsion of practical conscience, to the equi-possible category, and they will surely be those near the *extremes* of desiredness or counter-desiredness. Why should thought be given to a small misfortune, when a great one is rendered equally possible by the same choice of action? Or what significance has a small success, when a brilliant one beckons with equal claim of possibility? When all the sequels which the chooser has imagined for some course of action, and has not dismissed as impossible, are given by him equal possibility, it seems that only the best and the worst of this skein, the most desired and the most counter-desired, are relevant to his choice between this skein and any other, of which the same equi-possibility of its members is true. For since we suppose the chooser to recognize only one category of possibility, other than impossibility, there can be no difference of possibility between the members of different skeins. Each skein, if so, will be represented for the chooser by two sequels, one of them desired and the other counter-desired. The chooser is thus in the same formal position as the maker of a simple bet that some specified event will be realized. He has given himself anticipative access to one good outcome, at the price of accepting anticipative exposure to one bad outcome. Moreover, the chooser has chosen this particular *pair* of rival imagined sequels from amongst all the pairs which were offered by the available courses of action, wherever these pairs were nested in each other, that is, where the good sequel of one course was better than the good sequel of another, but its bad sequel was worse than the bad sequel of the other.

The psychic 'weighing' of a good against a *bad which is the price* of the good is a conception familiar to the economist. His essential object of study, the notion of *exchange*, is wholly centred upon it. To deem this psychic comparison, and the possibility of adapting the actions involved in exchange so that 'at the margin', equality is attained between the little more (or less) which might be given up, with the little more (or less) which might thus be received, unreal or impracticable, would be to deny to the economist his indispensable tool of thought, the heart of his theme of maximization of effect with given means. To balance a possible detriment, misfortune or loss against a success or gain whose possibility is brought into being, in the chooser's judgement, by this acceptance of the possibility of disadvantage, is merely to do what the economist supposes every individual to do who, for example, exchanges his leisure for his sustenance or (being, say, a baker) his surplus of bread for the brewer's surplus of beer. Exchange, in the economist's theory of value, is absolutely necessitated by specialization, where one man develops and employs the skills of the builder and another those of the tailor. There is evidently a further step to be taken by our chooser. Amongst those skeins of possible sequels, where the best overpowers the worst, he will seek the one where this out-matching is most decisive, and choose that course of action.

The formal business of the chooser's comparing of pairs of equi-possible sequels, one pair for each of his available action-courses, one sequel of each pair being the most desired and the other the most counter-desired of that skein, can be illustrated by another visual construction familiar to the economist, that of an indifference-map. On the west-east axis of a pair of Cartesian axes, distances are to represent, in terms of such units as we have considered, the loss or detriment represented by the worst sequel attributed to some action, and on the south-north axis, distances are similarly to represent gain or success. Thus any point in the north-east quadrant of the diagram will stand for the combined best and worst sequels deemed possible, out of those the chooser has imagined, for some one specific course of action. On such a diagram, an indifference-curve is the locus of all points which, for the chooser with his particular temperament, tastes and material endowments, are equally attractive or equally repellent. That is to say, such a curve contains, in its relevant segment, only points amongst which the chooser is indifferent. In our context, where greater supposed loss is represented by a greater distance from the origin eastward, and a greater supposed gain is represented by a greater distance northward from the origin, an indifference-curve will evidently slope north-eastward. We can conceive the entire quadrant to be densely covered by such curves, the whole constituting a map which Pareto, in his novel application of Edgeworth's original conception, called a 'photograph' of the individual's tastes. Pareto was concerned with a consumer's choice amongst pairs of *goods*, rather than pairs of which one member was in each case a counter-desired entity. In consequence his indifference-curves slope south-eastward. Evidently in our supposed diagram, any point on a curve lying 'north-westward' of another curve will be chosen in preference to any point on the more south-eastward lying curve. This means, of course, that of the two courses of action which correspond respectively to two points thus related to each other, he will choose the one on a curve lying further to the north-west.

For the economist, the indifference-map has proved itself a powerful and extremely versatile illuminant of all sorts of ideas. Its ostensible unrealism, such as the notion that an income-disposer could in principle consider 'every point' within reach of his income, despite the infinite number of such points, does not prevent this tool from being fertile in suggesting questions and theorems, and from offering convincing proofs of such theorems within the terms which the nature of the indifference-map imposes. For the purpose of my theme, its usefulness lies perhaps in more special extensions, rather than the general basis which I seek now to establish. These extensions are described elsewhere.* Here we must ask: What becomes of the notion of the best and the worst, the most desired and most counter-desired, of the sequels judged possible for any action, when we suppose the chooser to recognize imperfect possibility, rather than the simple absolutes of 'possible' and 'impossible'?

It seems evident that the most-desired sequel to which the chooser adjudges *some* possibility need not be the most desired of

* *Expectation in Economics*, Cambridge University Press, 1949, 1952; *Decision, Order and Time in Human Affairs*, Cambridge University Press, 1961, 1969; *Time in Economics*, North-Holland, 1957; and elsewhere.

those to which he gives *perfect* possibility. Beyond the most-desired of the perfectly possible sequels he may have conceived some which are still more desired, but are subject in his thought to some obstruction, so that to them he attaches some degree of disbelief or greater-than-zero potential surprise. Will the most interesting and arresting of all the non-excluded sequels necessarily be the most desired of those which seem *perfectly* possible? In what sense are we here using the term 'most arresting'? The relevant sense is that of capacity to influence choice, that is to say, capacity to afford anticipative experience. The good state of mind, the good state of imagination, may be attainable in the highest degree by means of a sequel whose slight impairment of possibility is overcome by its greater glory, its more brilliant content of imagined success. An idea surely even more convincing is the suggestion that practical conscience, the guardian of survival, will insist on attention being paid to sequels of less than perfect possibility whose realization would be a disaster, perhaps destroying the chooser's capacity for further action. I have elsewhere adopted the term *ascendancy* to mean the claim of any imagined sequel to be the representative of the skein as a whole at the desired or the counter-desired extreme. I shall term the respectively most ascendant of the desired and the counter-desired sequels the *focus-sequels* of the skein.

I have argued that the business of choice requires the chooser to treat the feelings and assessments which play a part in that business as in some manner, in some sense, each able to be located on some scale. Choice is an upshot of the *inter-action* of these feelings and assessments. If we are able at all to speak of degrees or intensities of such feelings, we are bound to suppose that the chooser associates an identifiable intensity of one feeling with an identifiable intensity of another. The feelings which take place in some present, which are the thoughts constituting that present, are directly known to him, they have the ultimate immediacy and reality beyond which nothing can exist for him. In the nature of things and in the Scheme of Things in which we are imprisoned, these intensities are as much known as anything can be. Thus it seems undeniable that what we might call molecular combinations of intensities of distinct kinds of feeling will take place in his thought. So far as such molecular packages leave any trace, they may thus present one feeling as a function, in the mathematical sense, of another. To suppose such functions to be *continuous* is undoubtedly to go beyond intuition and beyond experience. Nonetheless there does not seem to be any consequence of such a supposition which need deter us from taking advantage of the ease, efficiency and reach which it can confer on discussion. Some illumination of the business of choice can perhaps be gained by means of a formal representation in which we suppose some of the feelings and assessments involved to be continuous functions of each other.

Only three such measurables need be invoked. We suppose the chooser to have a scale for the desiredness or *value* of any imagined sequel of any action. This assessment refers to the content of that sequel, the tale it tells, regardless of the possibility, the degree of unobstructedness, that the chooser adjudges to it. Secondly, we suppose him to have a scale of *disbelief* or potential surprise on which he can locate any sequel regarding its possibility. Thirdly, we ascribe to him a scale of *ascendancy*, the power to arrest attention, exerted on him by any pair of mutually associated measurements on the other two scales. These three scales can be visualized as three Cartesian axes each at right-angles to the plane of the other two. In this frame we define an *ascendancy-function* of a form special and personal to the individual chooser, but belonging to a type whose broad character can be inferred. I assume that, of two positively desired or positively valued sequels of equal possibility, the more desired will be the more interesting to the chooser; also that, of two counter-desired or negatively-valued sequels of equal possibility, the *more counter-desired* will be of more concern to him than the less; and that, of any two equally desired or equally counter-desired sequels, the less possible will be the less interesting. If so, it will be natural to take the neutral sequel, a sequel neither desired nor counter-desired, as having zero ascendancy. Since we suppose that sequels judged impossible are of no concern to the chooser, all sequels located at entire disbelief will also have zero ascendancy. On these suppositions, the ascendancy-function will be a surface of two sheets, meeting in the plane of desiredness-disbelief in a line representing neutral desiredness. From this line each sheet will rise with increase of desiredness or counter-desiredness, but at each point on that scale, will fall with increasing disbelief to a zero level at entire disbelief.

Such a surface can be represented in two dimensions by a contour-map or equal-ascendancy-map, as illustrated in figure 16.1. Here desiredness is labelled G, disbelief is labelled y. G

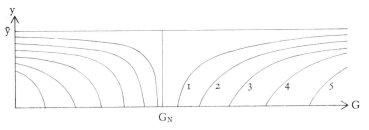

Figure 16.1. Curves labelled 1, 2, 3, 4, 5 are specimen equal-ascendancy curves. The two sheets of the ascendancy-surface are not in general symmetrical.

extends positively to the east and negatively to the west of a neutral sequel $G = G_N$. y extends from unobstructed possibility $y = 0$ to an absolute maximum $\bar{y}$ of entire disbelief, beyond which, no meaning is assigned to points on the axis of y. Within the region lying to the east of G_N and bounded by the lines $G = G_N$, $y = 0$, $y = \bar{y}$, the *equal-ascendancy curves* spring from the axis $y = 0$, and are traced north-eastwards to approach asymptotically the line $y = \bar{y}$. Within the similar region to the west of $G = G_N$, the equal-ascendancy curves slope north-westwards to approach $y = \bar{y}$ asymptotically. There is no reason to suppose any symmetry of the two sheets of the ascendancy-surface, except in their broad general type. In the positive region of G, an ascendancy contour lying to the east and to the south of another contour will represent the higher of the two degrees of ascendancy. In the negative region of G, ascendancy will increase towards the west and south.

Upon such an equal-ascendancy-map, indicated by a few specimen contours as in figure 16.1, we can super-pose a curve indicating the degree of disbelief adjudged by the chooser to this or that sequel of a *specific course of action*, such sequels being represented by their respective degrees of desiredness or counter-desiredness on the axis of G.

A possibility curve such as the one shown in super-position on an equal-ascendancy-map in figure 16.2 is of course uniquely

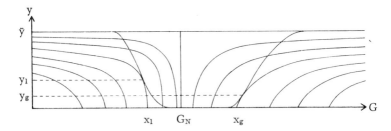

Figure 16.2. y_1: potential surprise of focus-loss; y_g: potential surprise of focus-gain; x_1: standardized focus-loss; x_g: standardized focus-gain.

special to a specific course of action within the chooser's reach. For a different course he will have in mind a different possibility curve. In this representation there is an anomaly which does not, I think, disable it from bringing into view some characters of the business of choice. If the imagined sequels of an action are deemed to be discrete (and such is plainly their nature, we cannot suppose the chooser to vary them continuously at all points of the calendar-axis in all dimensions of the space of affairs in which these sequels are described) then it is not appropriate to make the possibility curve continuous. However, this does not greatly increase the inherent artificiality of any such representation. Many imagined sequels of a course of action, widely diverse in character and valuation, may all appear to the chooser unobstructed within his knowledge and thus representable by points on the line of zero disbelief, the G-axis. Such a range will spread, as we have argued, on either side of the neutral valuation. If choice is to be meaningful and needful, however, this range of 'perfectly possible' sequels will be bounded. Beyond some point of positive valuation or desiredness, sequels still more desired will be associated with some positive disbelief, and it thus seems natural to think of the possibility curve as sloping north-eastwards in the G, y plane and eventually attaining the line $y = \bar{y}$ of entire disbelief. On the negative side of the neutral valuation the curve must by a parallel argument be supposed to slope north-westward, though by no means (except by extraordinary co-incidence) from a point at an equal distance from neutrality, nor symmetrically with the positive horn of the curve. There is no ground for supposing symmetry of the two arms of the curve. Within the degree of artificiality that such a representation may, perhaps, justifiably and usefully be allowed, we may suppose, in the positive range of valuations, that the equal-ascendancy curves will be convex north-westwards and the possibility curve convex south-eastwards. In such a case there will be a point of tangency between the possibility curve and some one equal-ascendancy contour, and this point will be a constrained maximum of the degrees of ascendancy of various positively-valued sequels. In the negative range of valuations there will be (in general, at a different level of ascendancy) a constrained maximum of ascendancy of the various negatively-valued, counter-desired sequels. With one further step, the two constrained maxima of the ascendancy-function can serve as the focus-points or focus-values of the particular possibility curve in question. The constrained maxima are (save by extreme co-incidence) at different levels of disbelief. By replacing each of them by that point which lies on the same equal-ascendancy contour but at zero disbelief, we have what can be called standardized focus-values, serving to represent the skein of possibilities of the particular choosable course of action, in the same way as this is represented by the focus-sequels in an absolute possible : impossible classification.

A formal representation on these lines, employing continuous functions, is somewhat less open to objection on the ground of this continuity, when the choosable action-courses are proposals to invest money capital in constructing business facilities, that is to say, in making tools, machines and productive systems, or in the sinking of mines or wells, or in networks for transportation or communication, or in buildings for any purpose. With such investment-proposals, the points on the axis of values will stand for hypothetical gains or losses in money terms, whose variation approximates to continuity in a practical sense.

A formal representation such as I have sketched can suggest and thrust upon us the difference of essential nature between two entirely contrasting postures of thought. The western traditional outlook is to regard any defect of knowledge as a failure to operate properly a machine which, if applied *à outrance*, can tell us everything relevant to choice. To suppose this is to suppose a deterministic world where 'choice' is predetermined and is not choice in the sense of a making of history, in the sense of an inceptive impulse not wholly governed by antecedents. To suppose, instead, that *possibility* in two roles or senses informs the nature of things makes choice effective. Our theme supposes that choice can be effective because of the void of time-to-come, the time of infinitely many possible variants, variants which are *unforbidden* by antecedent history, and thus possess a possibility belonging to the field, the *res extensa*. And it supposes that the thinking being assumes history-to-come to be awaiting his choice amongst skeins of *possibilities*, sequels of his choice of action whose possibility expresses his necessary unknowledge of what is unknowable because not yet existent.

In the next chapter some uses of the formal model to expose the consequences of our theme will be discussed.

)))
An axiom-system and some constructs
of potential surprise
(((

THREE TOPICS WILL engage us in this chapter. First we wish to elicit the essential nature of potential surprise by embodying it in an axiom-system of modest extent. Secondly, we wish to consider how the degree of potential surprise assigned to some outcome will be related to those assigned to distinct stages of the possible attainment of this outcome. Thirdly, some features and implications of the loss-gain indifference-map will be suggested. These topics will occupy respectively sections i), ii) and iii) of this chapter.

i) *Potential surprise as formal system*

An *axiom-system* or *geometry* is a set of propositions containing some finite sub-set $\mathscr{I}$ which can be called the initial propositions or axioms, from which the remainder logically follow. The system is essentially independent, self-subsistent and abstracted from all referends outside of itself. The entities and the relations involved in it are undefined. No question arises, therefore, of whether or not the axioms are true. Such a question would be meaningless. The axioms are required only to be mutually consistent, though elegance and simplicity will be served if they are also mutually independent. However, our purpose in proposing a particular system of this kind is to illuminate our theme of the nature of choice by exploring some possible properties of potential surprise. I therefore preface the statement of the self-contained abstract system suggested to me by the notion of potential surprise, by some explanatory statements and definitions.*

By a hypothesis is meant any suggested answer to any question, and by the contradictory of this hypothesis is meant the hypothesis that the suggested answer will turn out to be wrong. By *rival hypotheses* is meant two or more mutually exclusive hypotheses concerning the same question. By an *exhaustive set of rival hypotheses* is meant any set of heads under which the individual feels certain that the true answer to some particular question, the true outcome of some particular experiment, when it shall become known, will prove to be classifiable. Any set of rival hypotheses can evidently be made exhaustive by the addition to it of a *residual hypothesis*, defined as covering every particular hypothesis, whether the individual has formulated it precisely or not at all, having any character which would exclude it from classification under the hypotheses in the initial set. Of the seventeen propositions which follow, numbers 1–9, inclusive, are the *postulates* or *initial propositions*:

1. An individual's degree of belief in a hypothesis can be thought of as consisting in a degree of potential surprise associated with the hypothesis, and in another degree associated with its contradictory.

2. Degrees of potential surprise can be zero or greater than zero. No meaning is assigned to a degree of potential surprise less than zero.

Degrees of potential surprise are bounded above by that degree $\bar{y}$, called the *absolute maximum* of potential surprise, which signifies the absolute rejection of the hypothesis to which it is assigned, absolute disbelief in the truth of the suggested answer to a question or the possibility of the suggested outcome of an 'experiment'.

3. *Equality* between the respective degrees of belief felt by an individual in two hypotheses will then require, for its expression in terms of potential surprise, two statements, namely that some

* What now follows to the end of section i) is taken without alteration from my *Expectation in Economics* (Cambridge University Press, 1949, 1952) second edition, Appendix.

given degree of potential surprise is attached to both hypotheses, and that some given degree is attached to the contradictories of both.

4. The degree of potential surprise associated with any hypothesis will be the least degree amongst all those appropriate to different mutually exclusive sets of hypotheses (each set considered as a whole) whose truth (if it were established) appears to the individual to imply the truth of this hypothesis.

5. All the members of an exhaustive set of rival hypotheses can carry zero potential surprise.

6. When H is any hypothesis, the degree of potential surprise attached to the contradictory of H is equal to the *smallest* degree attached to any rival of H.

7. Let ^By_A be the degree of potential surprise assigned to a hypothesis B when ^Ay is the degree assigned to a hypothesis A, and let $^By_0$ be the degree assigned to B when $^Ay = 0$. Then ^By_A is not greater than the greater of ^Ay, $^By_0$.

8. Any hypothesis and its contradictory together constitute an exhaustive set of rival hypotheses.

9. At least one member of an exhaustive set of rival hypotheses must carry zero potential surprise. (But it is possible for all the rival hypotheses which are in any degree particularized or specified to carry potential surprise greater than zero, only the residual hypothesis carrying zero potential surprise.) The remaining propositions, numbers 10–17, are *theorems*.

10. From (8) and (9) it follows that the degree of potential surprise that a person associates with the contradictory of a hypothesis cannot be greater than zero unless the degree he associates with the hypothesis is zero; and vice versa.

11. From (5) and (8) it follows that a hypothesis and its contradictory can each carry zero potential surprise (notwithstanding that the contradictory may itself be capable of being resolved into two or more mutually rival hypotheses).

12. Let H be any hypothesis. Then from (6) it follows that the degree of potential surprise attached to the contradictory of H can-

not be greater than zero unless *every hypothesis rival to H* carries some degree of potential surprise greater than zero.

13. From (10) and (12), the contradictories of two rival hypotheses (i.e., two mutually exclusive hypotheses both concerning the same question) cannot both carry degrees of potential surprise greater than zero. For if H_A and H_B are two rival hypotheses, and the contradictory of H_A carries some degree greater than zero of potential surprise, this implies by (12) that H_B carries some degree greater than zero of potential surprise; but (10) implies that the contradictory of H_B cannot then carry any degree of potential surprise greater than zero.

14. From (3) and (13) it follows that if *equal degrees of belief* are felt in two rival hypotheses, the contradictories of both must carry zero potential surprise. The highest degree of *equal belief* which can be reposed in two rival hypotheses consists in assigning to both of them, and to the contradictories of both of them, zero potential surprise.

15. Let $^1H_1, ^1H_2, \ldots, ^1H_n$ be an exhaustive set of rival hypotheses concerning a first question, and let them carry respective degrees of potential surprise $^1y_1, ^1y_2, \ldots, ^1y_n$. Let Y be the degree of potential surprise assigned to a hypothesis ^2H suggested in answer to a second question. And let ^2y_i be the degree that will be assigned to ^2H if ^1H_i shall prove true. There are then two cases. First, if the ^2y_i are all equal, we assert that $Y = {}^2y_i$. For by (9) at least one of the ^1y_i, say ^1y_k, is zero, and by (7) Y will then be not greater than ^2y_k. Since the set ^1H_i is exhaustive, at least the degree ^2y_i must be assigned to ^2H. Thus $Y = {}^2y_i$.

16. Secondly, if the ^2y_i are *not* all equal, we assert that Y will be equal to the *least* degree which can be found amongst the complete set consisting of the *greater member of each pair* $^1y_i, ^2y_i$. For by (7), Y cannot be greater than the greater member of some pair amongst this set. But by (4) it will be the least amongst these greater members.

17. Let symbols have the meanings given them in (16). Then the individual will attach a degree *greater than zero* of potential

surprise to the hypothesis that when the answer to the first question shall have become known he will *reduce* the degree y of potential surprise he attaches to any hypothesis ^2H concerning the second question. For to assert the contrary would be to assert that there is some hypothesis ^1H_k to which the individual initially assigns potential surprise ^1y_k equal to *zero*, and that the degree ^2y_k of potential surprise which this answer to the first question implies for the particular answer ^2H to the second question is *less* than the degree y of potential surprise *initially* assigned, in *ignorance* of the answer to the first question, to ^2H. But this would involve a contradiction. For out of the pair ^1y_k, ^2y_k we have $^1y_k = 0$, and therefore by (2) ^2y_k is not less than ^1y_k. But if ^2y_k can stand for the greater of the pair ^1y_k, ^2y_k then it appears in the set amongst which, by (16) the least member is y, namely, the degree of potential surprise initially assigned to ^2H. ^2y_k cannot, therefore, be less than y.

ii) *Combination of conditional possibilities*

Let us suppose that the chooser envisages an enterprise whose outcome, he assumes, will be known at a named date in time-to-come. This outcome is represented in his thought by a continuous variable G, able to take positive and negative values which we can deem to be measured from a zero point, the neutral outcome, on the west-east axis of a Cartesian system whose south-north axis represents inverse epistemic possibility, namely potential surprise. At an earlier named date than that which will disclose the outcome itself, an intermediate taking-place, the chooser supposes, will indicate or suggest to him which one, out of a set of variant possibility curves now already formed in his thought concerning the outcome, he should adopt. Let us further suppose that each curve in this set assigns to any randomly selected value of G a different degree of potential surprise from that assigned by any other curve of the set, and that the lower the degree assigned by any curve to such random particular G, the higher will be the degree of potential surprise now assigned by the chooser to his *adoption* of that curve at the intermediate date.

Now the following question presents itself. The chooser has in mind a set of variant, rival, possibility curves concerning the outcome of the enterprise, amongst which a selection of one member will not be made until the intermediate date. Meanwhile the adoption of each of these curves carries some degree of potential surprise, and the less the disbelief which a particular curve assigns to any G, the greater the disbelief assigned to the eventual adoption of that curve. The chooser, however, needs now to define the form of a unique possibility curve for the enterprise. Evidently such a unique curve must be derived in consideration of the set of intermediate curves and the respective degrees of disbelief in their adoption. On what principle can we conceive such derivation to be performed?

My proposed solution of this problem* rests on considerations which can be best conveyed by a parable. Suppose that an explorer, in order to get from A to B on foot, must cross a line of mountains and a swamp. He will not be much surprised if a practicable route can be found on the mountain, but very much surprised if he succeeds in crossing the swamp. How shall he combine these two feelings to assess the possibility of his journey as a whole? This question as it stands cannot be answered by logic. It is a case for that intuition, heart-searching, introspection, which are condemned as 'unscientific' by those who exclude *res cogitans* itself and its operations from its own *res extensa*, Is there, for example, any manner in which we can suppose the two feelings to be added together? More than this: Is there any meaning to be found in any supposable result of such adding? If we were concerned with probabilities arrived at by some counting of cases, the orthodox procedure would be to multiply the two proper fractions together and obtain a smaller fraction. What sense could be read into such a result? The presence of the mountain does not make in any way *more critical* the difficulty of the swamp. It may reasonably be

* See *Expectation in Economics*; and *Decision, Order and Time in Human Affairs*.

suggested that the difficulty of the explorer's journey as a whole will present itself to him as the difficulty of its most critical, its most difficult phase. Let us return to the problem in its more general form. For any specified outcome of his enterprise, the chooser will discern many (perhaps in principle, infinitely many) paths of history which could lead to that outcome. Amongst those which he envisages in some symbolic detail, one such route will seem the least obstructed. Its adjudged effective degree of obstruction or difficulty will, I think, be that of its most critical phase. If so, the possibility which the chooser adjudges to a specified outcome of his enterprise will be that of the *most* possible route to this outcome, and the possibility of this route will be that of its *least* possible phase.

Let us examine this proposal of a rule of combination a little further in one respect before we apply it to the problem stated earlier in this section of the chapter. If the chooser can discern a number of variant routes to a specific outcome, a specific value of G, and if in particular several such routes appear to the chooser *equally* (though not *perfectly*) possible, will he not then have ground for according to the particular G a higher possibility (a lesser disbelief) than if only one route offered itself to his thought, even if this one route seemed as possible as the most possible of a skein of such routes? Let us remember that the members of such a skein are rivals. My reading of the question just posed is that the possibility afforded, in the chooser's thought, to the outcome cannot be increased save by his discerning some other route whose own assigned possibility is greater than that of the route he first considers. The mere piling-up of rival (mutually exclusive) routes does nothing to aid the possibility of their common goal. The only effect of such piling up is to recognize the incalculable plurality and diversity of things that can emerge from the time-void, not to give one particular ultimate phase or outcome a lesser degree of disbelief. If now we apply the rule to the initial problem of this section ii), the conclusion is that the potential surprise curve or possibility curve which the chooser can now trace, so as to take account of the forms of the intermediate possibility curves and the degrees of potential surprise respectively assigned to their adoption, will be the locus of points where the possibility assigned to some G *by* an intermediate curve is equal to the possibility of adoption assigned *to* that intermediate curve. Let us refer to figure 17.1.

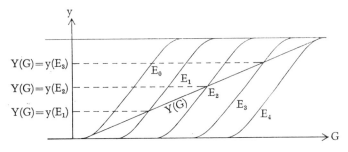

Figure 17.1. The curves labelled E_0, E_1, . . ., E_4 are members of a family of conditional potential surprise curves. The idea that at the intermediate date, curve E_i will be adopted as the unique curve assigning values of y to values of G, is itself in the chooser's present, assigned a degree of potential surprise y (E_i). The curve Y (G) entertained in this present by the chooser is the locus of points where potential surprise of adoption of E_i is equal to potential surprise assigned to G by E_i.

We suppose the chooser to look forward to two named dates in time-to-come. He counts upon a taking-place at the earlier of these dates which will indicate to him which one he should then adopt out of a set of possibility curves now already formed in his thought concerning an outcome G which he supposes will be known at the later of the two dates. He wishes now to determine that unique possibility curve, labelled y(G) in figure 17.1, which is implied, according to our rule, by the forms of the intermediate curves E_0, E_1, . . . , E_N and by the respective degrees of potential surprise which he now assigns to his adoption of them at the intermediate date-to-come. Each intermediate curve E_i is a *route* to any named outcome G_m. This E_i, considered regardless of its own possibility of adoption, assigns some degree say y_m of potential surprise to G_m. But if that degree y_m assigned to G_m by E_i is less than the degree $y(E_i)$ assigned to the adoption of E_i, then the effective potential surprise now assignable by the chooser to G_m by the route E_i is $y(E_i)$ and not y_m. This is so because, being confronted with two difficulties concerning the acceptance of the possibility of G_m, namely the difficulty *envisaged by* E_i and the difficulty of *adopting* E_i, our rule prescribes that the greater of these two difficulties is the effective one. On this same intermediate curve E_i, however, there will be some point where the two difficulties, the degrees of potential surprise assigned *by* E_i to G_m, and *to* the adoption of E_i, are equal, neither displacing the other. Such a point can, according to our rule, be accepted by the chooser as a valid judgement, according to his present knowledge, concerning the possibility of some value, say G_q, of the outcome. In the case we have supposed, where for G_m we had $y(E_i) > y_m$, the point of equality, $y(E_i) = y_q$, would lie to the east, further from the neutral outcome, $G_q > G_m$. Likewise if at G_m we had $y(E_i) < y_m$, then the point of equality would lie nearer to the neutral outcome. The consequence of our rule is illustrated in figure 17.1 for the special case where we suppose the intermediate curves E_i to be obtained from each other by mere translation along the G-axis, equal steps along the axis giving equal increases of $y(E_i)$. The argument of this section is set out in full in my *Decision, Order and Time*, chapter 24.*

iii) *A gain-loss indifference-map for enterprise investment*

The geographer's *contour-map* conveys on a plane diagram the character of a surface whose points are referred to three mutually orthogonal co-ordinate axes. The economist's indifference-map, constructed on the same principle, uses indifference curves each of which is the locus of all points representing some one and the same numerical value of one of three variables, let us call it z, and shows which pairs, say x, y of the other two variables correspond, accord-

* *Decision, Order and Time in Human Affairs*, where the argument somewhat elaborates that of *Expectation in Economics*.

ing to some suppositious continuous function $z = z(x, y)$, to this particular value of z. In our application the two argument variables are L, the standardized focus-loss which might be attributed by some business-man to a contemplated investment in some equipment-system for his business, and G the standardized focus-gain. We suppose the business-man to be able to determine which

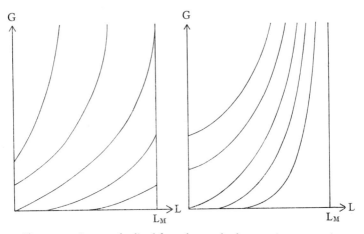

Figure 17.2. L_M: standardized focus-loss at absolute maximum, equal to the enterprise-investor's entire fortune.

pairs of numerical values (L, G) exert upon him some particular degree of inducement or counter-inducement to invest in the plant in question. We need not suppose him to put a numerical value on this inducement itself, but only to trace some specimen indifference curves. Curves representing different degrees of inducement will of course not inter-sect or touch each other, and if L is represented by west-east distances and G by south-north distances, an indifference curve representing a more powerful positive inducement to invest than another such curve will lie to the west and north of that other, as in figure 17.2. The indifference curves will all slope north-eastwards in the LG-plane since a larger focus-loss will need to be compensated by a larger focus-gain. Moreover, the slope of each curve seems likely to steepen towards the east, and the character of this steepening divides such investment indifference-maps into two types. At some point on the west-east axis a 'barrier' can be supposed to be erected at right angles to this axis, to represent the entire 'fortune' or total value of assets owned by the business-man or his firm. The eastward distance of this barrier from the origin stands for the greatest loss that he can suffer. According to his temperament the indifference curves may actually attain this barrier, and thus indicate his acceptance of the possibility of losing his whole fortune; or if he is more cautious, they will approach the barrier asymptotically. Some results attainable by inference from the notion of such a map are discussed in *Decision, Order and Time*, pages 162 and following and 277 to 296; *The Nature of Economic Thought*, pages 168 to 186; and in *Expectation, Enterprise and Profit*, pages 122 to 169.

)))
Symbols the necessary language of choosables
(((

My THEME HAS argued that the rival choosables are original arrangements by the chooser of elements suggested by reports from the field. The elements themselves are necessarily works of imaginative thought. The stream of impressions can be resolved by the chooser in many and perhaps indefinitely many ways into a scene made up *alphabetically*, that is, composed of characters, 'letters', forming a spelling system, as words, sentences, whole presentations of complex thought can be built of the letters of the alphabet. It is not evident that such building-blocks are dictated in form by the impressions. Such elements can be abstractions rather than imitations or borrowings of sensual impressions. Experience will test the validity of such elements, requiring each to serve repeatedly in resolving the ever-changing stream of impressions, reducing it to an 'intelligible' account of the state and transformations of the conjectured field. No imperious consideration seems to impose a unique form on such elements. The chooser cannot know what depth of detail is concealed from him by the impressions from the field and the 'reports' into which he interprets them. Can he know even that there is not in Nature, in the field which he infers from the reports, an infinite regress of levels or stages of analysable complexity? In the nature and origin of the elements themselves there is perhaps already a freedom for origination in the extreme sense, something essentially untraceable beyond the chooser's thought itself. But we suppose the elements themselves to be capable of arrangement in an endless variety of associations and sequences. They are not the pieces of a jigsaw puzzle capable of only one, determinate, arrangement, but the *tesserae* of free mosaic composition, pieces *set in a matrix of choices-to-come*. If such a nature and capability is ascribed to the elements, it seems evident that the histories-to-come, for whose composition they serve as well as for the interpretation of the reports from the field, must be symbolic, rather than literal statements of precise contingent detail.

The elements themselves, the *tesserae* of the infinity of possible mosaics, the letters of an alphabet capable of composing endlessly various sentential forms, are *symbols*. A language is of course a potential infinity of symbolic arrangements of symbols. In order to converse or to discourse, we need entities whose reference or meaning, whose *content of suggestion*, is in some degree invariant against changes of context and circumstance. But to form scenes and sequences of scenes as imagined sequels of choosable actions is to converse with oneself, to make discourse for one's own instruction. The first act of any kind of understanding is to classify. The names of classes are required to have permanent identities. These names are the boxes into which the classifiable miscellany of impressions, ideas or more complex thoughts are to be sorted. The elements which the chooser needs in order to understand the impressions from the field and in order to originate the possible contents of time-to-come are symbols, names of classes, boxes for gathering like with like.

To suggest a term and seek to define the need which its content is to fill, imposes on us the obligation to illustrate this term with examples. It will be difficult, in doing so, to avoid giving an impression of a class of thoughts altogether too restricted and special. We are speaking of the *elements of thought*, ineffably elusive and subtle, unseizable, incomparable, unanalysable, being themselves the ultimate knowables, the primary tools of the thinking being.

However, we are concerned with such elements in a particular use, where they are the means of tracing the sequential stages of unfolding of desired or counter-desired possible histories-to-come. They will thus be composed essentially of the thoughts attributable to others. Success consists in such thoughts. It is a judgement of the chooser founded on what he can discern of the judgements of others. The significant elements composing an imagined sequel of action will be bodies or systems of evidence, the fabric and circumstance of personal history or the history of those interests with which the chooser identifies himself, as servant, captain, manager, recorder, witness or priest.

The *elements* in their role as building-blocks of imagined sequels of choice will include such formal evidences as contracts of employment, appointment to office, business accounts, granting of patents, results of elections, solutions of formal problems, embodiment of inspiration in works of art or literature, scientific discoveries. This list, if it is accepted as illustrating the notion of element in our sense and in the role of the expressive medium of imagined history, shows clearly why elements must be symbols. A scientific discovery, yet to be made, cannot be specified in advance. How can the musical composer describe his score before he conceives or writes it, or the painter say with exactness what his painting will show or suggest? A language can express a limitless, unendingly extensible and proliferable variety of thoughts, feelings and imaginations, but a language is composed of symbols of somewhat stable and invariant suggestive content. The source of suggestions, which resides in a word or sentence, is somewhat determinate and is given by convention. The suggestions which it may inspire are by contrast unbounded in character and number. The elements in the sense with which I seek to endow this word, are the molecules, atoms or ultimate particles of a language.

We suggested in chapter 8 that there is no necessarily unmistakable sharp distinction and division between that part of the chooser's imagined content of time-to-come which he labels *action* and that part which he calls *sequence of action*. Action is something marked by the closeness with which the chooser feels that he can define what will take place in case he makes this choice, or that. Sequel is a skein of diverse and divergent possibilities proliferating with increasing remoteness of the time he contemplates.

Nonetheless, action itself can only be stated in symbols. The description of a business-man's proposed investment in productive equipment will specify classes of materials, operations and designs involved in constructing it. His intended recruitment of people will specify their skills and capacities but not their individual characters. There is perhaps a rich field of study in the relation of symbols, the names of classes of entities and operations, to the actualities which flow from decisions expressed in terms of these symbols. Does history depend partly on the exactness, the fineness and subtlety, of language, or its imprecision, vagueness and lack of power to discriminate? Yet this imprecision is essential in language's poetic power. The power of the poem is its power of suggestion. Words touch the strings of the reader's or the hearer's imagination. If language said explicitly all that could be said, if language could make *complete* statements of each theme in its entirety, language would lose the power to suggest.

)))
Elasticities of surprise
(((

I EARLIER SUGGESTED that the bounds of a skein of imagined possible sequels of some course of action must be defined as those two sequels which are respectively most desired and most counter-desired. When sequels are classified simply as possible or impossible, this definition presents no evident difficulties, provided the chooser can compare the desiredness of any two sequels. But if the chooser assigns degrees of possibility expressed as degrees of disbelief or of potential surprise, then he must specify some such degree which is the greatest that gives any hypothesized sequel a claim to the chooser's attention, or alternatively, he must contrive an ascendancy-function which makes the attention-arresting power of any sequel an increasing function of its desiredness and a decreasing function of its assigned potential surprise, so that two constrained maxima may be looked for which will with good reason be treated as the bounds of the skein.

The preceding chapters of my theme have made no attempt to specify the character or the mode of influence of those suggestions, derived by the chooser from the impressions he receives from the field, which he uses in originating the rival sequels ascribed as possibilities to some contemplated course of action. But there is one source of such suggestions, of which something can be said in general, namely, the comparison which we must suppose the chooser to make between the skein of sequels he had imagined when taking some particular course of action at an earlier time, and what seems according to his records and present observations to have followed since then in fact. On his scale of desiredness, points can perhaps be marked representing respectively the desiredness of the 'best' sequel, up to the present, and the desiredness of the recorded sequel, up to the present. If the latter much exceeds the former, a comparison can be made between the difference of these two degrees of desiredness, on one hand, and on the other, the difference of desiredness of the 'best' formerly-imagined sequel and the neutral degree. This comparison, it may reasonably be said, ought then to be treated by the chooser as the incentive and basis of a reconsideration of policy, for it represents the degree to which events have belied his expectations. Recorded relevant history for the time-interval since some enterprise (in a very general sense of the word) was conceived, has lain outside the bounds of what, in imagining that enterprise, he deemed possible in an acceptable degree. His judgement of possibility was therefore in some sense false, and the basis of knowledge and reason on which he made it needs to be re-examined.

Two conceptions employed by the economist can serve to illustrate this line of thought and give it precision. The question characteristically faces a business-man from time to time, whether he shall use money at his disposal for constructing some system of facilities in furtherance of his business, whether he shall invest in a more or less closely specified system of equipment, or not. He supposes that this plant will enable him to produce saleable goods in each of some series of intervals of time-to-come, and will require to be supplied in any such interval with means of operation, namely, materials, energy and human services. If, in any named interval-to-come, the goods to be then produced are taken to have a greater market value than that of the resources needed for operation, this excess, discounted to the chooser's present at a market rate of interest, is an item amongst those (one for each interval in the supposed life of the plant) whose sum is to be compared with the construction cost of the plant. Let us suppose, then, that the chooser's 'present' has advanced from the date of deciding on the plant, to the end of some such named interval of its life, and that the business-man then compares the realized trading revenue (sale proceeds of product less operating costs) of this interval with his initial focus-hypothesis of its amount. Let us write these various quantities as follows:

g the excess of the focus-hypothesis of (positive) trading revenue (in the named just-elapsed interval) over the neutral hypothesis.

Δg the excess of the recorded trading revenue of the interval over the focus-hypothesis.

j the focus *investment-gain* (total of discounted hypothesized trading revenues, less construction cost) from the plant.

Δj the amount by which the focus investment gain is revised upwards on account of the emergence of Δg.

The ratio $\Delta g / g$ is the proportion in which the focus positive trading revenue has been exceeded by the realized trading revenue. It expresses an out-turn which, by the meanings of our terms, must surprise the business-man. If we call Δg a gain of trading revenue, then $\Delta g / g$ is the proportionate gain of trading revenue which has emerged. Correspondingly, $\Delta j / j$ is the proportion in which his focus estimate of the eventual investment gain will increase as a consequence of the supposed surprising result $\Delta g / g$. The ratio of these two proportions has the form known as an *elasticity*. Here it expresses, as it were, the responsiveness of the business-man's judgement of eventual best-possible investment gain to a surprise in the amount of trading revenue recorded for one interval. A parallel construction could express the numerical increase in the focus investment loss which the business-man supposes would follow a given excess of realized trading loss over the focus-loss for the interval. Other such elasticities can be defined. For example, the business-man may now assume that in case of a proportionate gain $\Delta g / g$ of trading revenue in some named interval-to-come, he would increase his intended investment in similar plant, for some more distant interval, from I_n to $I_n + \Delta I_n$, so that the expression $\Delta I_n / I_n : \Delta g / g$ represents a responsiveness of *intended action*, that is, of *choice*, to a surprising recorded taking-place. Elsewhere I called such expressions *elasticities of surprise*. Many questions can be raised about their precise meanings and the business-man's possible modes of arriving at their numerical values. They are rather signposts on a road, serving to indicate its general direction, than detailed descriptions of the course of that road. I sought to elaborate such ideas in *Decision, Order and Time*, second edition, chapter xxx.

)))
'*The weight of arguments*'
(((

In his *Treatise on Probability*, in a chapter with the same title as
this present one, J. M. Keynes wrote:

> The question to be raised in this chapter is somewhat novel,
> after much consideration I remain uncertain as to how much
> importance to attach to it. The magnitude of the probability
> of an argument depends upon a balance between what may
> be termed the favourable and the unfavourable evidence; a
> new piece of evidence which leaves this balance unchanged,
> also leaves the probability of the argument unchanged. But
> it seems that there may be another respect in which some kind
> of quantitative comparison between arguments is possible.
> This comparison turns upon a balance, not between the
> favourable and the unfavourable evidence, but between the
> absolute amounts of relevant knowledge and of relevant
> ignorance respectively.*

This passage is in several respects a surprising sequel to Keynes's
introductory chapter. There he explains that

> In most branches of academic logic, such as the theory of the
> syllogism or the geometry of ideal space, all the arguments
> aim at demonstrative certainty. They claim to be *conclusive*.
> But many other arguments are rational and claim some weight
> without pretending to be certain. The terms *certain* and
> *probable* describe the various degrees of rational belief about
> a proposition which different amounts of knowledge author-

---

* *A Treatise on Probability* by John Maynard Keynes (Macmillan 1921)
chapter VI, page 71.

ize us to entertain.

When we argue that Darwin gives valid grounds for our accepting his theory of natural selection, we do not simply mean that we are psychologically inclined to agree with him. We believe that there is some real objective relation between Darwin's evidence and his conclusions, which is just as real and objective, though of different degree, as that which would exist if the argument were as demonstrative as a syllogism. We are claiming, in fact, to cognize correctly a logical connection between one set of propositions which we call our evidence and which we suppose ourselves to know, and another set which we call our conclusions, and to which we attach more or less weight according to the grounds supplied by the first.

The reader of these passages and of the rest of Keynes's chapter I will get from them, I think, the impression that what distinguishes a *probable* from a *demonstrative* inference is the lack, in the former case, of some propositions which would complete the set of premisses and render it capable of supporting a demonstration. There is no suggestion, in these introductory remarks, that some of the evidence may be positively adverse. It seems even more difficult to reconcile the term '*rational* belief' with a body of evidence containing items which contradict the conclusion, than to reconcile it with evidence which is merely insufficient. Thus Keynes's chapter VI seems to go beyond what chapter I has prepared us for. May it not be fairly suggested that when a body of evidence, to which we are looking for support for some conclusion, contains items which seem to oppose that conclusion, the relation between the evidence and the conclusion is more naturally to be taken as that of judgement and not of logic?

The first paragraph of Keynes's chapter VI, quoted above, speaks of 'quantitative comparison' between arguments, and refers to 'the absolute amounts of relevant knowledge and relevant ignorance'. Even in his opening chapter Keynes speaks of the degrees of rational belief which 'different amounts of knowledge' authorize us to entertain. Is logic, then (whether providing certain or only probable inference) a matter of *quantity* of knowledge? A logical argument is a *structure*, its validity depends on relations of meaning, not in any sense on 'how much' knowledge there is. It seems as if Keynes in speaking of 'evidence' must have had in mind something different from the axioms, postulates, initial propositions, premisses, whatever we elect to call them, of a proof such as those of Euclid. Was not Darwin's evidence for natural selection a matter of cumulative suggestion? Piled-up examples are 'evidence' in a loose and conversational sense, or in that of a court of law, where it is called circumstantial evidence. No doubt we can speak, with some warrant in vernacular usage, of a body of evidence whose *items* (not logically interlocking propositions) can be enumerated as being larger or smaller. But this does not offer a clear interpretation of the first paragraph of Keynes's chapter VI. Yet that chapter is highly intriguing and suggestive. Can the notion of the 'weight of arguments' throw light on the epistemic interval?

It will be my contention that possibility, being the absence of fatal obstacles within the chooser's knowledge, cannot be intensified or reinforced, in any sense which affects the action-chooser, by the discovery of many variant routes to the situation whose possibility we are concerned with. If the action-chooser has in mind an imagined path of history-to-come which leads to a desired situation, and which is unobstructed by anything in the chooser's knowledge, then the attainment of that situation is for him possible, and the conceiving by him of other imagined paths, also unobstructed, which also lead to it, will not make that possibility more effective in sanctioning anticipations (enjoyment or satisfaction by imagination) which require this possibility. If the chooser hesitates to accept as possible a result or situation which is unobstructed along one path, until he has multiplied for himself the ways in which it can be looked on as unobstructed, then *possibility* does not mean for him what, in my theme, I am supposing it to.

In this light, *weight of argument* does not seem to have a part to play in a theme which proposes to consider, as the operative epistemic variable, possibility instead of probability. Yet in elaborating this theme we must draw encouragement from the style and spirit of Keynes's book as a whole and of chapter VI in especial. For the phrases used in that chapter point unmistakably to an intuitive or instinctive sympathy with judgement rather than logic. Keynes wished to achieve formalism and 'objectivity' in his treatment of the manner of filling, as I wish to say, the epistemic interval. Formal treatment, the diamond facets of logical rigour, are intellectually beautiful, they cut the hardest materials. Beauty is the proof-deviser's ultimate clinching satisfaction, the classic intellectual glory. But it is the desire for a perfect formalism which, it seems to me, has impelled theorists to mistake the nature of unknowledge. It goes against the grain of Western man's whole history and ambition to recognize an ultimate stop to his progress towards 'control' of his affairs. The inspired creative power, the *original* Promethean gift, original in its continuous power of perhaps *ex nihilo* contribution to history, which drives the human affair along, is incompatible with foreknowledge. The gift of choice (if choice means anything worthwhile) denies us the gift of knowledge of time-to-come. For how should there be knowledge, in every present moment, of what men are about to *originate* in the extreme sense, to draw from the void?

Yet Keynes's intuition of the weight of arguments seems to me to correspond to something different from the question of the epistemic standing of specific hypotheses. Keynes does not ask himself (it is no concern of his) whence come the 'conclusions' which are to be supported by this degree or that degree of 'rational belief'. But this for us is a central strand in our theme. The nature and source of the rival choosables appear to be something into which economists have never thought to enquire. We have elected to suppose that they are work of imagination supplied with materials by suggestions from the field, but not governed in its use of these suggestions by any determining antecedents. The *richness*

131

of suggestion can evidently play a part in the origination of history. Keynes thought, in his chapter VI of the *Treatise on Probability*, that 'an accession of new evidence increases the weight of an argument'. Perhaps we may gloss this statement by saying that he would suppose a chooser to give 'more audience' to an argument which now rests on 'more evidence'. Instead of this, the effect I would ascribe to 'new evidence' is that of increasing the richness of suggestion on which the chooser can draw in imagining rival sequels to any contemplated course of action. New evidence has its effect, I would say, on the content of a skein of imagined sequels, on the modes and directions in which sequels, all ascribed to one and the same initiating action or use of specific resources, diverge from each other, or are distanced from each other, in form and character, rather than on the possibility of particular sequels, unless this new evidence is radical enough to introduce obstacles not discerned before.

Let us try to draw these foregoing threads together. Keynes seems in chapter VI of the *Treatise on Probability* to be appealing to a different notion, or a different aspect and mode of employment, of 'evidence', from that with which he launches his enterprise in chapter I. In chapter I he is embarking on the search for a 'new kind of logic', may we say, a sort of 'field of force' by which a set of propositions might support a conclusion. This would be something quite different from that structural, 'tangible' or 'visible' solid support which a set of propositions gives to a conclusion entailed by them. When a conclusion is entailed, it merely shows us the entailing propositions, as a whole, in a different light. The conclusion is of their essence and inseparable from them. This new kind of logic, if it deserved the name of logic, would surely still have to rely on formal characters discernible in the 'evidence' and in the conclusion. It would still be *form*, rather than quantity, which was the essence of the matter. In chapter VI we are in a different milieu of ideas. There we are invited to consider 'quantity of knowledge'. Is not this the posture of Counsel in a court of law? The 'evidence' which he adduces depends, for its operative force, on a series of 'ifs'. Here, he says in effect, we have a mass of details which could be seen as belonging together, could be seen as parts of a unity, if we were to assume the guilt of the accused. 'These details' he may be deemed to say, 'would be a striking co-incidence if they did not have some unifying thread of intention or of compulsion, entertained or experienced by the accused, running through them. If only we assume his responsibility, we shall be relieved of this sense of a tale without a fully articulated plot. Let us suppose it to be really a complete story. This will give us aesthetic and intellectual satisfaction'. If he can make the pile of 'items in search of a plot' larger, he may make more oppressive his hearers' desire for some receptacle into which to put all the items tidily. The strength of that desire is the strength of his case. The case is a suggestion, its strength is its power of suggestion, that power is partly a matter of quantity, of the number of illustrated pages in a book which could be joined in meaning by a particular plot. But 'suggestion' is an invitation to engage in figment, not a summons to acknowledge truth. The resulting figment may embody truth. It is not bound to do so. Figment stands in essential contrast to what Keynes had in mind when he said: 'In the sense important to logic, probability is not subjective'.

The Keynes of chapter VI might, I think, have been a little more accessible to my theme than the Keynes of chapter I.

)))
A meaning for 'calculable risk'
(((

My theme makes unknowledge of the sequel of present choice of action a logical consequence of a policy of thought concerning the nature of history, of time itself. If history is made by men, it cannot be foreknown. Yet in order to draw, from their imagination and commitment, actual reports from the field; in order to turn *dunamis* into *entelechy*; men must choose action and engage in its actuality, they must, in the conversational meaning of the word, 'take risks'. Risk is a word we have so far eschewed because its conversational meaning differs essentially from the one that actuaries and theorists of probability have imposed upon it. For them, risk is *calculable*. How can that be calculable, which is a manifestation of unknowledge? The answer is that *risk* in the actuary's sense is an aspect of a practical means, in one particular type of context, of eliminating unknowledge and its effects to some degree. That type of context is the one where relative frequencies of the occurrence of counter-desired outcomes from numerous and continuing trials made under stable conditions can be calculated and legitimately projected. When the actuary speaks of *risk* he is concerned with knowledge of a kind, not perfect but of high practical value. In illustrating the notion of relative frequencies we referred to a tossed coin or to dice thrown from a box. In life at large the 'systems' which yield frequency-tables consist of the policy-holders of insurance companies, and the repeated trials made with these systems arise from their members' exposure to accidents, misfortunes or mortality. As an individual the policy-holder cannot know when a destructive event will happen. But loss occasioned by it in money, whenever it may happen, can be commuted into a known regular payment of premiums. For the insurance company the business of writing policies is what we may call a *divisible experiment*. What matters to the insurance company is its experience as a whole of its policy-holders in their premium payments and in their claims on the company. This encompassing experience, suitably classified by the kind of exposure to misfortune of the policy-holders of various kinds and circumstances, provides the company with the necessary conditions for deriving and applying frequency-tables. Thus the divisible experiment made continually by the insurance company becomes a *seriable experiment* from the standpoint of the policy-holder, whose affairs are merged with those of the others so that all share equitably in bearing a roughly knowable burden of loss.

'Risk' then, in the actuary's terms, is calculable, but it names an aspect of a procedure for eliminating or mitigating what in ordinary conversation we mean by 'risk'. The risk which cannot be insured against, the risk arising from irremediable unknow-ledge, is not calculable in the sense in which the risks handled by insurance companies are.

For there are what we may call *non-divisible non-seriable experiments*. It is plain that if the action whose sequel is in question is of a kind which *by its nature cannot* be repeated, there can be neither derivation of frequency-ratios nor use of them by projection on to stretches of time-to-come. Such actions, such non-divisible or *crucial* experiments, are an essential and unexcludable part of the Scheme of Things. Most radically of all, there are what we may call *self-destroying experiments*, in which the performance of the action, the making of the experiment irreversibly destroys the conditions which are its essence. If I wish to know the effect upon me of reading some work of literature, I must read it. Having done so, I cannot regain my ignorance of it. To hold an election, to fight a battle, whatever the outcome may be, will affect the world in ways which cannot be expunged. What sense can it make to speak of calculated risk in relation to a self-destructive experiment?

Unknowledge confronts the action-chooser in the form of a *plurality of rival imagined things deemed possible*. Some of these are thoughts which lift his heart and some are ones which sink it. The price of access to desired imagined sequels is awareness of counter-desired sequels, thrust upon thought by practical conscience intent upon survival. Choice throws open the gates of anticipation to the good and to the bad. The question the chooser must ask himself is: How bad is the worst that this choice makes possible, is its contemplation too high a price for the hope of high success? 'Risk', in the conversational sense which has been stolen from it, is measured by the badness of what is possible, not by a 'probability' assigned, without any explicable meaning, to the contingency of a particular outcome of a crucial, non-repeatable experiment. We cannot climb the mountain to get above the fog. But we can seek the edges of the plain within which the course of things seems free to turn and swing.

When we are told that some choice of action or policy is a 'calculated risk' we are justified in asking *what* has been calculated. If the reckoning aims to find some stop beyond which misfortune could not carry the enterprise, some limit to the degree of crippling of action in remoter time-to-come which could result, this is at least the attempt to answer a meaningful and relevant question. If the claim is to calculate 'the chances' of this result or that, we are entitled and obliged to ask a number of questions:

1. *What question is answered* by a calculation of 'the chances'? (If the question that is answered concerns possibility, why does the claim speak of 'chances'?)

2. What *procedure*, what sequence of steps, does this calculation consist of? *How* is the calculation performed?

3. What eventual report from the field, what recorded result will tell us whether the calculation was correctly made and whether it gave the right answer? If there has been a success, and this outcome was given a chance of one-in-two, was that a right calculation? Why was the chance not given as one-in-one?

If 'calculated risk' refers to some feeling that we ought not simply to dismiss the epistemic interval, but ought to be ready to consider 'possibility' of a kind or degree other than the perfect, more especially when counter-desired possibilities are in question, we ought still to be concerned with possibility in the sense that our theme has proposed, possibility meaning essentially the adjudged absence of fatal obstruction, and expressed inversely as degrees of disbelief or doubt, rather than with 'chances' that have no referend to which we can point, no operational or ostensive definition. We may feel inclined to refer to those 'degrees of rational belief' which are assigned to individual hypotheses on some grounds other than a *distribution* of 'portions of certainty'. But how are such 'degrees of rational belief' themselves to be calculated? They seem to be inevitably as subjective as assigned degrees of possibility.

Calculation requires data. These may be strongly attested by reports from the field, or they may be the terms of an abstract problem invented purely for the sake of its beauty, subtlety or difficulty; or they may be suggestions offered by the News in the light of the Scheme of some action-chooser engaged in following out possible sequels of a choosable action. But if the data are insufficient for demonstrative proof, or if they do not all rest on evidence from the field but are inventions of the chooser filling gaps in that evidence, then calculation cannot lead to demonstrative truth about anything outside the individual's thought. If 'calculable risk' is meant to suggest that calculation can be a substitute for evidence and not merely an exploitation of it, then this phrase is a muddle and merely covers a pretence.

)))
Enterprise, *or action in pursuit of imagination*
(((

My theme has been involved in the unavoidable dilemma
which faces any attempt to express a line of thought of one's own.
The power of words to give thoughts a conveyable form depends
upon convention. The usage adopted, practised and ceaselessly
tested in exchange of discourse by the native speakers and writers
of a language gives to each of its terms a bundle of more or less
intersuggestive, related and coherent packets of content or strands
of meaning. The endeavour to use some term in the service of an
idea which has, at least for its proposer, something of his own
invention, some glint of original conception and novelty, necessarily throws upon this term a light from an angle unfamiliar to
other users. The term is obliged to share to some degree the novelty
which it seeks to express. It has to express that somewhat novel
meaning, or construction of ideas, by suggestion, it has, if it is to
succeed in its task, to induce in the hearer's or reader's thought a
leap of intuition imitating that of the proposer of the supposedly
original thought. Thus the bundle of meanings of this term is
added to, *its effect as a whole* is somewhat changed, enlarged, or
charged with a force which is new to it. Is it not then obligatory
upon a writer who has more than once, in the course of his argument, sought to deflect in a slight degree the established direction
of several terms, to systematize his proceedings and set up something resembling a table of relationships amongst such terms? The
notion of a private etymology must seem exorbitant and even
arrogant in some degree. Its justifying intention is surely quite the
opposite, namely, to defend and regularize what might otherwise

confuse and alienate his readers.

My proposal is to show that a few ideas whose mutual involvement is the essence of my theme can each be seen from several
distinct aspects, or with different distributions of emphasis over
its various faces, and that these aspects of one and the same basic
notion can sometimes be illuminated by using different terms for
one and the same idea. The questions that are posed by the theme
of choice can, for example, be mostly linked to the term *rival
choosables*. We have asked whence and how the rival entities, to
one or other of which, expressly or by default, the chooser on
some occasion is obliged to commit himself, are brought into
being in his thought; what essential nature is prescribed for them
by our election of a notion of choice which makes it *effective*, an
ultimate source of history, rather than a passive and sterile link
between pre-destined states of affairs; how a distinction is to be
made, within the structure of each choosable, between *action* and
sequel; how choosables of the complexity that effective choice
seems to imply, can be compared by the chooser in a manner
which recognizes all this complexity. When we consider the
notion of a choosable, seen in this light of the effectiveness of
choice, from the especial standpoint of the action involved in it,
we may appropriately call it an *enterprise*. This term puts emphasis
on the idea of commitment and on that of a burden, of a special
sort, involved in this commitment, the burden, namely, of
accepting in advance the outcome whatever it may prove to be,
and of accepting it while it is unknown. Every choice, we may say,
is an enterprise, on a small or large scale, in a matter ostensibly
slight or apparently momentous. But to use the term enterprise
brings out an aspect of *effective choice* of which political economy
seems to have been little aware.

Enterprise suggests another essential aspect of choice, namely,
that action requires resources. If it were not so, there would be no
need for choice of action. Evidently we are here using the term
resources in an encompassing sense. If the chooser had unlimited
powers of attention capable of simultaneously coping with ques-

tions endless in number and variety; if his physical stamina was unlimited, his topographical space for movement boundless, the flows of energy from Nature and the quantities of materials at his disposal superabundant, then he could do all things at once and, perhaps we may say, he could at one time think of all things to do. This picture is the extreme opposite of the human condition. Resources are only to be called such if they are *scarce*, that is to say, if they must be directed to the attainment of one end *or another*. The chooser earns that name because he can find in himself and his surroundings only so much of the gifts of intellect and concentration, of moral effort and resolution, of physique, and of the power to out-reach by imagination his pressing weariness and despondency; can find in his possession only such-and-such of the tools and systems, the sources of chemical or biological energy, the materials, and the power of persuasion to elicit the aid of others. It is these things of which he must say, I commit them to one task, I cannot commit them to another. The chooser is the thinking being who in thought can do this *or* this, who for a particular course of action can see some imaginable sequels blocked but must acknowledge an endless variety of sequels which are possible, and who can at most set bounds, in terms of desiredness or counter-desiredness, in terms, that is to say, of valuation, to any such skein of hopes and anxieties. Enterprise is action in pursuit of imagination, and only imagination can supply the incentive and immediate reward for that act of rendering *possible* some bad and counter-desired things, as the price of rendering *possible* some good and desired things. And the assignment of possibility is the act of the chooser himself, impelled by his practical conscience, his instinct to desire survival. It is thus illuminating, I think, to say that the rival choosables are rival *enterprises*.

The term enterprise tends a little to stress that aspect of the business of choice of action, which shows it as an acceptance of unknowledge, or as I have tried to urge, as an *exploitation* of unknowledge. Unknowledge liberates imagination which seizes and occupies the void of time-to-come. The business of choice, however, is a response to imperious practical needs. Choice of conduct insists on being made, either with deliberation and conscious assessment, or by default. It can, with essential justice as my theme seeks to suggest, be looked on as a gamble, as a *relishing* of unknowledge, of the diversity of possibilities. But it can and must be looked on also as the pursuit of ends. The chooser as gambler can be conceived to say 'Let me see what this move will bring, its variant hopes and anxieties provide the exciting and motivating tension'. But the chooser as would-be survivor, as would-be attainer of particular ambitions, must be supposed to say 'Let me see what move will best launch towards my goal an expedition which, after this inception, must steer by its own observations'. This view of choice as the conceiving of *ends*, even if they are formulated in widely encompassing and general terms, and an attempt is made to render them imaginatively possible by a choice of action which includes the desired end within its skein of possible sequels, may better be labelled *policy*.

Like enterprise, *policy* is a complex and subtle notion. In the context of business, politics or diplomacy, in that of scientific research or even of artistic creation, *policy* tacitly recognizes uncertainty. If conduct and endeavour could guarantee the attainment of highly specific ends, there need be no employment of a word which suggests *hopeful action*, and *flexibly suggestible* action.

To adopt a policy is not to prescribe in detail a course of action stretching to remote calendar dates, a course to be followed through thick and thin. *Policy* is a term suggesting that some general principles are formulated to guide choices of action in time-to-come in pursuit of ends prescribed in more or less exact or general terms; principles, however, envisaging some constraints on the character of the actions to be adopted or of the means to be employed. *Policy* has an eye to means as well as ends, and may dissolve the distinction between them; but *policy* implies also a recognition that when a policy is launched, only the existing and the desired situations are clearly seen, and that the path from one to the other will be the work of choices-to-come. Policy recognizes unforeknowledge.

Enterprise and *policy* each implicitly accepts a view of the human predicament, a view of the nature of choice of action. Choice is deemed by each to be effective, to make a difference, yet to be unable to specify uniquely the sequel of any choice. For enterprise, however, the void of time is a liberation, a field of play where the rules are not fully given and known from the outset but are endlessly to be discovered and even invented. For policy, the endless plurality of possible sequels of action is as insistent a condition as it is for enterprise, but a hindrance and disadvantage unless the aims of policy are formulated with an extreme appreciation of the depth of originality and resource that humanity commands, so that one aim of policy is to attain a new platform from which policy itself can be re-formed.

Analysis, dissection, the urge for insight, for the ever-more-penetrating resolution of a reified term or hypothesis into its elemental bits, has its eternal dangers. We have adopted and sought to define a set of terms: choice; course of action; sequel; bounded but infinitely numerous skein of sequels imagined and not discernibly obstructed; horizon; symbolic encapsulation of action or of sequel; enterprise; policy. We have sought to emphasize the essential mutual inter-necessity of these terms, the involvement of the meaning of each with the meanings of the others, even the ultimate unreality, the illusive artificiality of the effort to separate and distinguish them into individual building-blocks of the theme. It is, if any claim can be justified, the theme as a whole that must achieve some intuitive conviction, if any such is to be attained. Thought is integral. What is 'the present', if time-to-come is not an idea which is entertained in the present and belongs to the content of the present? What are the reports from the field, until interpreted and assimilated to a scheme of the field? What is 'the News' if shorn of its rich suggestiveness and provision of 'elements' for the work of imagination? What are the choosables, if not the chooser's thoughts? What reduces the ineffable plurality, subtlety, complexity and eternity of things to manageable symbolic representations, if not the chooser's judgement, grounded somehow in experience yet able, if our theme is luminous, to transcend experience with *original* powers? Does the notion of *beginning*, of *ex nihilo*, outrage the scientific outlook? Then, what makes good the continual evacuation of space by the expanding universe, if we accept the steady-state cosmology, or in the big bang hypothesis, what accounts for the primeval atom? Is the notion of 'the void' escapable?

The elemental parts of such a theme as here attempted are not 'parts' like those of a machine. They are better suggested by analogy with the views of the nature of light, where 'particle' and 'wave' can each respond to some one kind of question.

)))
The formal, *and the nature of choice*
(((

THERE ARE THOUGHTS, suggested by experience, which none-theless are too far abstracted from any particulars, too general in what they can accommodate, too fundamental, too absolute, to be regarded as descriptions of the field, the *res extensa* supposedly lying outside the thinking being's thought. They more nearly present themselves as descriptions of thought itself, and we may say that the experience which suggests them is the experience of thinking. They are thoughts whose content is their form, their naming of intuitively seized relationships. These thoughts are primitive, that is, unanalysable, indefinable in other terms. They are the ultimate means of defining all else. At the outset of my theme, I sought to identify with each other the formal aspects of thought, transience and time. Thought, the only *direct knowable*, is a transient, something in which arrival and departure are an essential, inseparable unity. The transience of thought is our direct intuition of time, it is what, in the first place, we mean by time. All that we know is thought, and all thought is in the present, the solitary moment of actuality, the moment-in-being. All that we know is what comes to us in this momentary present, all that we know is the News. This conception is a formal one. It illustrates the notion which, above, I have tried to fix as the formal. However, since this conception reflects our experience, albeit our most in-escapable and basic experience, our very experience of being, must we not say that it is a means of description, an idea with a referend outside itself? In this conception, are we not unifying the formal and the supposedly natural, are we not seeking to *inform* in a particular way the field, the source of our impressions, and thus to give the field a part of the nature we see in it? If so, it seems that the purely formal, thoughts which are thoughts only and not thoughts about impressions from outside, can, nonetheless for this absoluteness and purity, illuminate the supposed field and give insight into it? Do we here find a bridge from *res cogitans* to *res extensa*, unifying in some sense their natures?

Paradoxically the formal is very real to us. A classic example of the formal is the indefinable notion of *successor*. The whole numbers as a class can be so arranged that each is the successor of another, so long as we confine ourselves to this class. This notion appears at first to have a meaning quite independent of the notion, the intuition, of time. Yet may we not say that a successor is an entity which, belonging to some class, is the member of that class which we come to *after* coming to some particular other member. After? This is time. The calendar-axis, the imagined formal 'space' which accommodates the inferred consequences of our intuition of transience, is basic to our descriptions of the supposed field, it belongs to our *Scheme of the field*. It seems that the formal contributes in an essential way to our notions of the natural.

This idea is exemplified in our theme. In it, we have inferred, from a formal conception of time, a particular and paradoxical character of choice. If choice is to be deemed capable of making a difference, if choice is to be deemed effective and originative, it follows that what will be chosen, and when it will be chosen, is essentially, ineluctably, unforeknowable. If by choosing we can *originate* history, then others in times-to-come can also give to the course of things impulses now unforeknowable which will affect the sequel of the choice we make now, Choice, if effective, has an effect which we can describe only as a skein of seemingly unobstructed imagined sequels in a landscape of other imaginable, but obstructed and impossible, sequels. The nature of choice and the nature of history would then flow from a formal intuition, a notion of thought and time. It is said that we cannot 'anticipate Nature', that all knowledge must come from observation. But this observation need not be only the receipt of impressions from 'the field'. The dividing frontier between *res cogitans* and *res extensa*, between thought and report, between examination of our most essential intuitions, with their implications, on one hand, and examination of the field beyond thought, on the other hand, seems to be bridged by our need to interpret the reports, to formulate from them intelligible News, in the light of formal notions of thought, transience, time and succession.

)))
Is there a logic of uncertainty?
(((

THE FORMAL CONDITION for the presence of uncertainty in a
person's thought is the presence there of a question to which he
cannot exclude all except one answer. In any attempt to treat my
theme exhaustively, this statement would call for much refinement, but I shall here take it to be sufficient. The answers which
must be excluded in order to make the one answer certain include
not only those which the person has already thought of, but any
which, for all he can tell, may still occur to him. Unless, therefore,
the question belongs to a context where explicit rules enclose the
matter, it may be possible to say that certainty is unattainable. Our
problem can be seen to open out disconcertingly. What is the
proper *reach* of a question and its answers? Suppose the question
is: Who was Shakespeare? What system of component questions
will give full expression to this summary question? Are we asking
about his ancestry to unlimited degrees of remoteness, about his
personal history or his genetic inheritance? Within any one of
these, or other possible questions suggested by the first, there will
be terms whose interpretation allows of great or indefinite
diversity. Only in a subject-matter purely formal and abstract, it
might seem, could we be sure of such limitation of meaning that
one answer could be seen as the sole possible one. What then is the
character of such a subject-matter which makes exclusion of all
but one answer possible? It is the rigid completeness of rules or
principles which not merely delimit but *constitute the essence* of the
subject-matter, which gives us certainty. In Russell's conception,
though not in Gödel's, mathematics is such a field. The game of

chess, but not the game of politics, is such a field. How can such rigid completeness of rules or principles be attained, not in a game or a work of the formal imagination, but in the world of sensation and emotion, even in the world of experimental science? Only by skeletizing such a world. Only by the setting-up of classes and categories which essentially are abstractions, constructs, artefacts, inventions, works of originative thought. Logic works with abstractions, not with what impinges on our eyes and ears, not with what goes on in the emotive reality of life. For certainty, for indefeasible knowledge, we must represent the sensual and emotional experience by a formal system. The certainty we may thus attain will relate to the formal construct and not to the experience itself, but this is the best that we can do, it is *all* we can do. If my premisses can so far be accepted, one conclusion seems already within reach. The logic that carries us from axioms to theorems in science or in the practical disciplines does not inform us directly about the world of sense impressions or emotions, the world of the actual signals and pressures, but only about some formal scheme on to which we seek to map the direct experience. Can we then say that some one scheme is the only one which can serve the purpose? What ground can we possibly have for saying so? If the question we seek to answer concerns the experience and not some symbolic account of it, it seems plain that no answer given by such a symbolism can be treated as fundamentally the sole non-excludable answer. The gap between experience and logic is one which logic cannot bridge. To suppose that it could would be, I think, a category-mistake. If the world of experience is altogether cut off from logic, a logic of uncertainty could itself exist only in an abstract system. However, in order to cope with life, we in practice identify the world of experience with some one or other of the abstract systems that suggest themselves. Such systems are not mere variant means to one and the same end. The motive that we ascribe to the adoption of one system can be essentially different from the one offered for another. Some systems implicitly appeal to results which will be reported at the end of some interval of time-to-come. How are such reports supposed to bear on choices, decisions, which must be made at the threshold of the interval? To claim that reported outcomes can bear on the choices whose outcomes are in question is to subvert the nature of the human condition, to de-nature time itself and to abolish the meaning of past and future, save as segments of an axis whose points are in all senses co-valid and whose contents are equally accessible, from every such point, to the knowledge of the decision-makers. 'The present' in such a conception loses its *specialty*, its solitary unique actuality, its sole and exclusive possession and representation of *what is*. Instead of modelling the world of experience, this conception adopts, sometimes even tactily, the assumption that men have perfect knowledge of the content of time-to-come. That is to say, it *abolishes* time-to-come. Yet there are some whose nerve is not quite equal to this. They wish for a means to do away with ignorance without claiming knowledge. There is, they suggest a 'guide of life' which will tell us what to do, will justify and establish this recommended course, will provide meaning for the claim that this course is the wisest one, yet will concede that 'In Metaphysics, in Science and in Conduct, most of the arguments, upon which we habitually base our rational beliefs, are inconclusive to a greater or less degree'. These are the words of Maynard Keynes on the first page of his *Treatise on Probability*. If the arguments are inconclusive, what ground have we for relying on them?

But let me re-phrase this question. What ground have we for relying on them to produce, in time-to-come, at the *end* of the interval at whose threshold we stand, particular results *now specified*, which will be *then* reported as fact? There is a quite different, an essentially and fundamentally different, way in which we can, not abolish uncertainty but exploit it. The motive for making a choice of action is, I would say, to act upon the one thing which is most directly knowable to each individual, which is plainly the most accessible and the most vital to him, his immediate state of mind. Choices are resolutions, they are commitments of moral resource to some scheme of steps of action, and the desired and attainable effect of this commitment is to give the chooser access to desired imaginations of history-to-come, access to the contemplation of imagined sequels, rendered epistemically possible by his act of choice. If the action-chooser could find in his knowledge of the nature or existing posture of things some fatal objection to all such sequels except one; if, that is to say, he felt himself to possess certainty concerning the reports which, in time-to-come, would reflect the outcome of his present choice, knowledge would have taken the place of hope, the flight of thought would be destroyed. Is it conceivable that every imaginable sequel of present action except one, when that sequel can stretch to the remotest time-to-come in which the chooser feels any concern, can be subject in the chooser's thought to a fatal objection? If experience of life does not give forcefully enough the answer no, I think there is an argument which gives it conclusively, on that argument's own terms. If choice is a *beginning* in the extreme sense of an influence not itself entirely shaped by antecedents, if choice sets up in affairs and in history a ripple which is in some degree *ex nihilo*, then choices are not foreknowable, the circumstances by which choices made in time-to-come will affect the sequel of any present choice are unforeknowable, and that sequel itself, therefore, cannot be foreknown. The *if* upon which this argument rests is the *if* of non-determinism. But what would *choice* be, in a determinist world?

Let us then come to the question: If an argument is not conclusive, if it is not a rigorous demonstration of logical necessity, if it does not exhibit premisses and conclusion as two aspects of one and the same unity, what is its value to us, why should we rely on it? At the head of the first chapter of his *Treatise on Probability* Keynes quotes Leibniz: 'J'ai dit plus d'une fois qu'il faudrait une nouvelle espèce de logique, qui traiteroit des degrés de Probabilité.' The *Treatise* is Keynes's endeavour to fulfil this demand, or at least to establish the rightness of the goal.

To reason successfully from stated premisses to a conclusion is to show that there exists a unity, a thing held in thought, of which the premisses are one aspect and the conclusion another, these two aspects being, in the nature of this thought, *inseparable*. If our mind is powerful and penetrating enough, we cannot think of the premisses without thereby thinking of the conclusion, 'Both grow in one'. If the reasoning is *not* conclusive, this means that the unity of premisses and conclusion does not exist; it means that there is a gap, a void. If we were allowed to invent, to introduce from somewhere outside of the evidence which we actually possess, some additional premisses, perhaps that gap could be bridged and the conclusion rigorously attained. But then we have to ask: May not some different conclusion be able to suggest itself, for which some different additional premiss would serve to bridge the gap and thus provide us with a rigorous demonstration of a conclusion contradictory of our initial one? May there not, indeed, be an infinity of conclusions, different from our first proposal, which could be attained by additional premisses which we could invent? If so, on what ground could we prefer one rather than another of these conclusions? Could there be any such ground which we could claim to be a logical one? Evidently we cannot tell what sort of thing Leibniz's 'new sort of logic' might be. It would be rash indeed to say that no such formal rules can ever be found. We may readily admit that a body of evidence, which is not sufficient to demonstrate one conclusion and thus refute all contradictories, may nonetheless carry powerful suggestions. What are suggestions? They are the touching of the keys on the keyboard of personal experience, of structures of explanation which the individual has built up for himself, by some resemblance or reminiscent impression reported in the present. They depend upon his own individual history, the detail and exact content of his educative life. Suggestions are evocations of a *personal* response. They call upon the resources of imagination, of originative power, they may perhaps be seen as the condition *sine qua non* of a beginning in the sense I sought to outline, a thought whose occurrence, but not whose form or content, springs from some report from the supposed external world. If so, those who wish for a logic of probable inference would surely dismiss them with the con-demnatory word 'subjective'.

)))
Index
(((